W.G. Grace

Pocket BIOGRAPHIES

Series Editor C.S. Nicholls

Highly readable brief lives of those who have played a significant part in history, and whose contributions still influence contemporary culture.

Pocket **BIOGRAPHIES**

W.G. Grace

Donald Trelford

Sutton Publishing

First published in the United Kingdom in 1998 by
Sutton Publishing Limited · Phoenix Mill
Thrupp · Stroud · Gloucestershire · GL5 2BU

British Library Cataloguing in Publication Data

A catalogue record for this book is available from the British
Library.

ISBN 0-7509-1836-5

Typeset in 13/18 pt Perpetua.
Typesetting and origination by
Sutton Publishing Limited.
Printed in Great Britain by
The Guernsey Press Company Limited
Guernsey, Channel Islands.

CONTENTS

'I write about the famous champion Grace,
Most wonderful of all the Cricket Race'

'Century'

CHRONOLOGY

1848	**18 July.** Born near Bristol
1857	Début for West Gloucestershire (aged nine)
1862	Nearly dies of pneumonia
1863	Chosen for All England XI (aged fifteen)
1864	First century (170 not out) v. Sussex. Scores 50 on first appearance at Lord's (aged sixteen)
1866	First double century (224 not out) v. Surrey (aged eighteen)
1868	First match for Gloucestershire. Scores 134 not out for Gentlemen at Lord's. Scores hundred in each innings for first time. Registers as medical student in Bristol
1869	Elected member of MCC
1871	First player to score over 2,000 runs (2,739) in season, including ten centuries. Father dies
1872/3	MCC tour of Canada and United States
1873	Marries Agnes Nicholls Day. Enrols as student at St Bartholomew's Hospital, London
1873/4	Tours Australia on honeymoon
1874	First player to achieve double of 1,000 runs and 100 wickets in season
1875	Highest number of wickets in season (191)

1876	Scores 400 (not first-class match) and two triple centuries, including 344 for MCC, highest ever score in first-class cricket
1879	Qualifies as doctor
1880	Début Test century (152) for England v. Australia. Brother Fred dies
1884	Mother dies (match abandoned)
1886	Scores century and takes all 10 wickets for MCC v. Oxford University
1888	Captains England for first time
1891/2	Captains England in Australia
1895	**May.** First player to score 1,000 runs. First player to score 100 hundreds
1896	Innings of 301 aged forty-nine
1898	Jubilee game at Lord's on his fiftieth birthday; public appeal raises £9,000.
1899	Last game for England.
	Retires from medicine.
	Leaves Gloucestershire.
	Joins London County Club and moves to Kent.
	Daughter Bessie dies of typhoid, aged twenty
1903	Captains England at bowls against Scotland
1905	Son W.G. jnr dies of appendicitis, aged thirty
1906	Last game for Gentlemen, aged fifty-eight (scores 74)
1908	London County Club is wound up
	Retires from first-class cricket (aged sixty)
1914	Last club game for Eltham, aged sixty-six (scores 69 not out)
1915	**23 October**. Dies at Mottingham, Kent

GRACE
ABOUNDING

W.G. Grace is one of the very few Englishmen who can be immediately identified by his initials alone. His beard and gargantuan frame are still easily recognised, 150 years after he was born and 83 years after his death. His fame in his own lifetime was such that only Queen Victoria, William Ewart Gladstone, and possibly Florence Nightingale, could match it. Ronald Knox once suggested jokingly that Gladstone and Grace were the same man. For a country doctor from Gloucestershire, who played sport when his duties allowed, celebrity on such a scale without the benefit of mass communications is remarkable. How did he achieve it? And what sort of man lay behind the beard?

W.G. Grace created modern cricket and was its first great practitioner. By his genius and force of personality he converted a pastime into a national institution. The structure and organisation of the game as it is played today, and the central arts of batting, were set by this singular man in the second half of the nineteenth century. He is without challenge as England's finest cricketer, arguably our greatest sportsman of all time. Only Sir Donald Bradman, of Australia, stands comparison as a batsman, and Grace was a consummate bowler too.

His bare figures are extraordinary: 54,896 runs, including 126 centuries; 2,876 wickets and 875 catches in a first-class career spanning 44 seasons from the age of sixteen to sixty. In addition, he played a great deal of club cricket rated less than first-class in which he scored another 91 centuries. According to some estimates, he may have scored 100,000 runs in all forms of cricket, a record that will probably never be surpassed. Most of those runs were scored on pitches so rutted, uneven and dangerous that modern players would refuse to bat on them. Because of this, statistical comparisons with batsmen in other eras cannot reasonably be made, except to note that no other player, with the possible exception of Bradman, was so far and away better than his contemporaries.

His lasting effect on the techniques of batting was explained by the next greatest exponent of the period, K.S. Ranjitsinhji, later Maharajah of Nawanagar:

> He turned the old one-stringed instrument into a many-chorded lyre. The theory of modern batting is in all essentials the result of W.G.'s thinking and working on the game. . . . I hold him to be, not only the finest player born or unborn, but the maker of modern batting.[1]

What marked Grace out from all other players, before or since, was his power and strength, derived from his great size. He had the advantage of an unusually long reach and went aggressively after the bowling, the faster the better, making some phenomenal hits. But he did not rely on power alone, being the first player to master the art of steering the ball skilfully between the fielders and judging a run. He had been well coached by his family in the basic techniques of defence, on which all batting ultimately depends. He was the first batsman to play both forward and back with equal facility. He had that remarkable coordination of hand and eye demonstrated by all great performers down the years. He also showed unflinching courage in facing fierce bowling on dangerous wickets.

He was a natural sportsman, with an exceptionally good eye for shooting, and shared his family's skill on horseback – until, in later years, at nearly 20 stones, he grew too heavy for any horse to carry him. He loved all country pursuits, especially beagling and fishing. In later life he took up bowls and became captain of the England team.

In all these exertions he showed an almost superhuman energy and stamina well into middle age. He was constantly on the move. Although the railways had arrived, travelling round the country from ground to ground in those days must have been a gruelling experience, and he also had a medical career to maintain. He once stayed up all night with a difficult confinement and next day scored a double century. *Wisden* said of him when he died: 'When he was in his prime no sun was too hot and no day too long for him.'[2]

He came to maturity at a time when the construction of railways and tarmacadam roads made it geographically possible for cricket to become a national sport. This coincided with the growth of industrial towns with a population hungry for new forms of mass entertainment. A rural pastime, previously associated with gambling, thus became a commercial business.

Grace single-handedly changed the economics of cricket by making it a sport with mass appeal. He saved the MCC, the governing body of cricket, by throwing in his lot with the newly created county system, which was under its control, rather than with the groups of itinerant mercenaries who had dominated the game when he started. Being a man who liked to have it both ways – and he generally succeeded in this – Grace also managed to run his own travelling circus, the United South XI, from which he made a great deal of money, while also playing for Gloucestershire.

Grace was nominally an amateur at a time when the social distinction between gentlemen and professional players was supposed to be maintained rigorously. Yet he became seriously rich through cricket, earning an estimated £1 million at modern values during his career. There are countless stories of his greed, bordering on venality. The game turned a blind eye to this hypocrisy because, as the editor of *Wisden* wrote, 'Nice customs curtsey to great kings and the work he has done in popularising cricket outweighs a hundred fold every other consideration.'[3]

He was also guilty of gamesmanship on a shamefully grand scale, craftily bending the rules where he could, intimidating opponents and umpires, sometimes refusing to be given out. Lord Hawke wrote:

> He would stretch the laws of cricket uncommonly taut in his own favour, but nobody bore him a grudge.[4]

The first part of his lordship's comment was more true than the second. He and his brother, E.M. Grace, himself a gifted cricketer, used to chatter non-stop on the field, indulging in the form of harassment known in our day as 'sledging', first attributed to the Australians. W.G. narrowly escaped prosecution for hitting a boy with a stump in one of his bursts of temper.

The Graces were no orthodox Victorian plaster saints. Socially they were country squires, middle-class professionals rather than gentlefolk, with rough manners and few airs and graces. Even though he was a medical man, W.G. does not appear to have subscribed to the Victorian maxim that cleanliness is next to godliness. More than one wicket-keeper noted that the back of the great man's neck was none too clean. The Graces exuded the physical self-confidence of countrymen and did not waste time on inner questioning. They were muscular Christians, but with more emphasis on the former than the latter.

For all his ruthlessness on the cricket field, away from it Grace seems to have been a gentle sort of giant, modest about his own achievements, gruffly shy in conversation, kind to women and children (his granddaughter remembers plaiting his beard as she sat on his lap).

The snootier elements at Lord's regarded him as a simple soul, a country bumpkin, an overgrown schoolboy, not notably bright (he took eleven years to qualify as a doctor), who represented all the silent virtues of Victorian manhood. He drank and smoked little and belonged to a generation for whom sex was for procreation, not recreation.

Europe was aflame with revolution in the year of his birth, just as it was to be engulfed in war at his death sixty-seven years later, but there is little trace of these upheavals in the details of his life. It is remarkable, in fact, how hermetically sealed from the outside world Grace seemed to be. The only recorded instance of W.G. commenting on the public affairs of his time was a letter he wrote to the *Sportsman* in 1914, saying it was time to abandon the cricket season so that the players could 'set a good example'[5] by going off to war.

The name of W.G. Grace does not appear in the history books of Victorian England, yet he was not only one of the most famous but also one of the most influential figures in the social history of his time. Of the eminent Victorians who shared his fame, none enjoyed the same public affection. Sir Arthur Conan Doyle, who probably prided himself more on having once claimed Grace's wicket than on writing the Sherlock Holmes stories, wrote:

> He had many of the characteristics of a great man. There was a masterful personality and a large direct simplicity and frankness which, combined with his huge frame, swarthy features, bushy beard and somewhat lumbering carriage, made an impression which could never be forgotten. Few men have done more for the generation in which they lived, and his influence is none the less because it was a spontaneous and utterly unconscious one.[6]

The pressure of his fame, with the public demanding success every time he went out to bat, must have been a heavy weight for Grace to bear, especially as he grew older. It may also have driven him on and inspired him to greater achievement. It was possibly this burden of expectation, as well as his natural competitiveness, that made him argue with umpires. He did not want to disappoint his fans by getting out too soon. It was literally true, as he is said to have told an official who was trying to dismiss him, that 'people have come to see me bat, not to see you umpire'. He was idolised as cricket's first superstar, a century before the phrase was invented, acquiring an almost mythic status in the eyes of his contemporaries.

Yet he received no honour from the Crown. He should have been cricket's first knight, an honour that went to Sir Jack Hobbs half a century later. He might have become a lord at the end of his life if the Prime Minister, Herbert Asquith, had implemented his plan to flood the House of Lords with Liberal peers to create a majority there. According to Asquith's grandson, the late Lord Bonham-Carter, Grace's name was on a list of putative peers found among his papers, along with those of Ranjitsinhji, C.B. Fry and H.G. Wells. But the constitutional crisis of 1911 was resolved and Grace was not required to exchange Lord's for the House of Lords. In any event, his political sympathies, in so far as they are known, were probably Conservative, as he was said to have 'detested radicals'. He may have been influenced in this opinion by his mother's recollections of the Reform Act riots in Bristol at the time of her marriage.

There are surprisingly few memorials to our greatest national sporting hero, the most famous being the Grace Gates at Lord's, bearing their famous understated inscription, 'The Great Cricketer'. Even though a commemorative game took place at Lord's on the 150th anniversary of his birth in July 1998, it was dedicated to the memory of Diana, Princess of Wales, whose association with cricket was rather less well-known. Tony Blair removed a portrait of W.G. from over the fireplace in 10 Downing Street where it had been lovingly placed by his predecessor, John Major.

His death in 1915 was overshadowed as a national event by the news of the dead and wounded from the First World War. The war confused and depressed him and he confessed to being made more afraid by the Zeppelin raids on London than he had ever been by the fast bowling of F.R. Spofforth and C.J. Kortright.

The effect of his death, even at a time of international cataclysm, seemed to mark the end of an era, as the journalist A.G. Gardiner captured in his book, *Pebbles on the Shore*:

As I stood on the platform . . . devouring the latest war news under the dim oil lamp, a voice behind me said, in a broad rural accent, 'Bill, I say, W.G. is dead'. At the word I turned hastily to another column and found the news that had stirred him. And even in the midst of world-shaking events it stirred me too. For a brief moment I forgot the war and was back in that cheerful world where we used to be happy, where we greeted the rising sun with light hearts and saw its setting without fear. In that cheerful world I can hardly recall a time when a big man with a black beard was not my King.[7]

T W O

A FAMILY
AT PLAY

William Gilbert Grace, known as Willie to his mother, Gilbert to his friends, the Champion or the Old Man to his contemporaries, but for ever to the world as 'W.G.', was born on his mother's thirty-sixth birthday, 18 July, 1848, the fourth of five sons and the eighth of nine children of Dr Henry Mills Grace and his wife Martha. His grandfather, also Henry Grace, had been a footman and later butler at Ashton Court, Bristol, home of a baronet, Sir Hugh Smyth. Grandfather Grace was said to be Irish and, according to a possibly biased witness in a court case at the time, 'a great, coarse, potbellied, unwieldy man, wholly deficient in the grace of God'.[1]

It says much for Henry Mills Grace, this dubious footman's son, that, despite a deprived family background, he was able to cross the rigid social boundaries of the time and grow up to be a doctor.

This required great application, a quality Henry Mills had in abundance. He worked first in his native Bristol as a surgeon's apprentice, the usual testing ground for medical students to see if they could stand the sight of blood, and then at St Thomas's and Guy's Hospitals in London. He became a member of the Royal College of Surgeons in 1830, at the age of twenty-two.

The following year he married Martha Pocock, whose father George was one of Bristol's great eccentrics. George Pocock ran his own academy in the city and also went around as an itinerant evangelical preacher, barnstorming the local mining community from a tent mission he pitched in their midst and waging a private war with the official Methodist authorities. He had a passion for building box-kites and kite-propelled carriages, a subject on which he wrote a book, *The Aeropleustic Art*, and raced them between Bristol and Marlborough at speeds of up to 20 mph, sometimes with his daughters aboard. He is reputed to have overtaken the Duke of York's coach on one of these excursions, which prompted the Duke to invite him to Ascot to display his various forms of kite-propelled transport. Legend has it that he once strapped Martha, the mother-to-be of W.G., into a chair attached to a set of kites and then flew her, hazardously but without mishap, over the Avon Gorge.

After his marriage to Martha, Dr Henry Mills Grace settled into a medical practice at Downend, thereby crossing the few miles from Somerset to Gloucestershire, with significant consequences for English county cricket. Downend was then a separate village but is now absorbed in the suburbs of Bristol.

Dr Grace was strong of limb and character, a renowned horseman who rode to hounds with the Duke of Beaufort and did his medical rounds on horseback or by gig, covering many miles in a day on bad country roads. He and Martha lived for nineteen years at Downend House, where they raised their nine children, of whom all five boys were to follow their father into medicine and three went on to play cricket for England. The children came in the following batting order: Henry (1833), Annie (1834), Fanny (1838), Alfred (1840), Edward Mills (1841), Alice Rose (1845), Elizabeth Blanche (1847), William Gilbert (1848) and George Frederick (1850). After that Dr and Mrs Grace declared the innings closed. The three future

England Graces, all known by their initials, were
E.M., W.G. and G.F.

As his family grew, Dr Henry took on a wider
range of medical duties, presumably to boost his
income, including that of surgeon to the local
colliery. In this role he attended a mine disaster in
1845 and amputated a leg without anaesthetic while
the injured miner chewed on his pipe. He was also
surgeon to the Royal Gloucestershire Hussars,
consultant to Mason's Madhouse, the local lunatic
asylum, and parish doctor to the poor. He was
described in an official report as 'an intelligent
practitioner and a gentleman of benevolent and
considerate feelings'.[2]

Dr Henry was also obsessed with cricket, an
interest he indulged whenever the opportunity
arose, often rising at dawn to play for three hours
on Durdham Common before his daily rounds
began. Encouraged by his eldest son Henry, who
had become enthused with the game at school, he
laid out a pitch at home at Downend. W.G. can
hardly have played on this, since the family moved
to a bigger house up the road when he was only
two, though his first recollection is of holding a bat
at that age.

At the new house, known as Chesnuts (without the middle 't', for reasons which have never been explained), Dr Grace and his brother-in-law, Uncle Pocock, chopped down some apple trees in one of the garden's two orchards and laid out a practice pitch that has become part of cricketing legend. They removed turf from the nearby hedgerows, then mowed, rolled and watered it lovingly at every opportunity. 'I cannot remember', W.G. wrote later, 'when it was not in a condition worthy of a first-rate club'.[3] The bowling would have been mostly round-arm, as the game was then in transition from under-arm to over-arm delivery.

Cricket had only been formally legalised, along with other outdoor sports, in 1845, three years before W.G. was born. The obstacle had been the gambling closely associated with the sport from its rough beginnings in the early eighteenth century at the Hambledon Club on Broadhalfpenny Down in Hampshire.

In later life W.G. recalled his practice sessions in the garden as the key to his cricketing prowess:

I used to chalk a wicket on a wall and get a stable boy and one or two youngsters from the village to join

me. So I got some sort of practice – sometimes with
a broom handle instead of a bat . . . I consider that a
great deal of my quickness of eye is due to the fact
that the boys with whom I played bowled a very large
proportion of fast underhand 'daisy cutters' which
used to jump about in a most erratic way and needed
a lot of watching.[4]

It is worth noting that two cricketers of later
generations, Don Bradman of Australia and Brian
Lara of the West Indies – perhaps the only two who
could be truly compared in genius with W.G. – also
learned the game as boys by playing for hours on
end in the garden with golf balls and sticks that left
them with exceptional eye–hand coordination.

Grace would have had little time for those who
say cricket is essentially a matter of natural talent
and flair. 'I have had to work as hard at learning
cricket as ever I worked at my profession or
anything else,' he said.[5] The collective family
practice sessions, involving the whole Grace family,
plus the servants and the dogs, demonstrated an
obsession with cricket and a huge enjoyment of the
game for its own sake. The shrieks and the laughter
from the orchard can almost be heard down the
years. W.G. recalled in his memoirs:

I was born in the atmosphere of cricket. My father, who was a keen sportsman, was full of enthusiasm for the game, while my mother took even more interest in all that concerned cricket and cricketers. When I was not much taller than a wicket, I used to wonder what were the hard cuts, leg hits and long drives which my father and brothers were constantly talking about. As far back as I can remember, cricket was a common theme of conversation at home.[6]

The cricket orchard at Chesnuts was bounded by a wall on one side and a water-filled quarry pit on the other. They rigged up a canvas sheet on three poles to act as wicket-keeper. W.G. wrote of this makeshift domestic arena:

We had only to step out the house and begin to play. . . . It was not much of a pitch, nor was it full size, but it was sufficient to teach the rudiments of the game. . . . My father, my brother Henry and my Uncle Pocock practised at every spare moment, and we youngsters fielded for them from the moment we could run about.[7]

The family rule was that grown-ups had fifteen minutes for batting and the children five. At least one nursemaid collapsed with exhaustion after throwing balls to the young Graces. A local man called Alf Monks was hired to do some of the bowling, with a two shilling piece or half crown balanced on top of the stumps as an incentive for him to bowl straight. The family dogs, called Don, Ponto and Noble, two pointers and a retriever, became fearless and athletic fielders of the ball. A neighbour noted their remarkable anticipation of where the ball would go – except when the unpredictable E.M. was at the wicket.

When W.G. first joined in, probably around the age of six, his brother Henry would have been twenty-one. E.M., who was seven years his senior, was seen as the family star until W.G. overhauled him in his late teens. E.M. was the most striking personality in a family hardly devoid of character. Four wives and eighteen children (thirteen by his first wife and five by his second) bear eloquent testimony to a life lived to the full. A contemporary account described him as 'overflowing with cricket at every pore, full of lusty life, cheerily gay, with energy inexhaustible'.[8] He was also one of the outstanding cricketers of the nineteenth century. Had he not been overshadowed by W.G., his lasting fame would be greater. He was the shortest of the

Graces and perhaps for that reason, or because he practised as a child with a bat too big for him, he cultivated a cross-batted swipe to leg which horrified the purists, though they had to concede that he became one of the cleanest and most prolific hitters in the country. His prodigious talents emerged at Canterbury when he was twenty-one, scoring 192 not out with some ferocious hitting, then taking all 10 wickets in the second innings. In the 1863 season he scored over 3,000 runs in all forms of cricket. It was his fielding, however, as well as his unorthodox hitting, that became legendary. He fielded close to the wicket at point and took catches almost off the blade of the bat at such speed that nobody knew where the ball had gone.

A volatile man with a short fuse on his temper, E.M. did not suffer fools gladly and more than once he responded to a comment from the crowd by putting his bat aside and physically attacking the culprit. On another occasion, however, when a summons for breach of promise was served on him while he was batting, E.M. exhibited remarkable coolness: he simply gave the paper to the umpire and completed a fifty. He went on to play first-class cricket for Gloucestershire until he was fifty-five and was the club secretary from its inception for thirty-nine years. Two years before his death, when he was sixty-seven, he took 119 wickets for the Thornbury club side.

The need to compete with older and stronger brothers would have been a powerful incentive for W.G. in his youth. A glimpse of the brothers' coming rivalry is provided in a letter Martha wrote to the great Nottinghamshire batsman, George Parr, known as 'the Lion of the North', when he was putting together an England squad for the first overseas tour in the 1860s. It is one of the most famous letters in English cricket, revealing her shrewd technical knowledge of the game. E.M., she wrote, is a 'splendid hitter and most excellent catch'. However, she added presciently that she had 'a younger son, now twelve years of age, who will in time be a much better player than his brother because his back stroke is sounder, and he always plays with a straight bat'.[9]

Dr Grace snr's obsession with cricket moved to a larger stage when he formed a cricket club at neighbouring Mangotsfield, which he later merged with the West Gloucestershire Club. Eventually, in 1870, he formed Gloucestershire County Cricket

Club, then filled the team with members of his own family. Founding a cricket club was not just a matter of paperwork in those days, but of hard physical toil, morning and night, nursing a playable pitch and cajoling the locals into helping to flatten the outfield. Though lacking the talents of his famous sons, Henry Grace was an enthusiastic cricketer, batting right-handed and bowling with his left. He died in 1871, just before his sixty-third birthday, having caught a cold out hunting and sat up all night with a patient. The *Lancet* wrote of him: 'Few better horsemen ever rode to cover.'[10]

Whether his wife Martha picked up her own cricketing knowledge from her brother and her husband at the family practice sessions in the garden is not known. Richard Daft, one of the period's greatest batsmen, said of her: 'She knew ten times more about cricket than any lady I ever met.'[11] Later, when she followed her sons around the country's cricket grounds, she was accorded great respect by the players. When the pros were playing for Gloucestershire at Clifton, they used to raise their caps to the old lady as she sat in her carriage by the pavilion, and some were summoned to be told exactly why they had got themselves out. A contemporary overheard her saying to W.G. after he had lost his wicket through a bad shot at Oxford University: 'Willie, Willie, haven't I told you over and over again how to play that ball!'

She kept scrapbooks of her sons' performances and always insisted that they send her a telegram with their scores at the end of each day. Several observers noted the courtesy she was always shown by her sons. The esteem in which this woman 'of magnificent physique and indomitable will'[12] came to be held was demonstrated at her death in 1884, when W.G. and E.M. were playing for Gloucestershire against Lancashire at Old Trafford. The Lancashire captain, A.N. 'Monkey' Hornby, abandoned the match to allow the Graces to return home.

Even today it seems an extraordinary gesture and the match remains the only one ever abandoned for the reason which the Gloucestershire scorer solemnly wrote in the scorebook – 'owing to the death of Mrs Grace, the mother of the famous cricketers'. Had Gloucestershire been playing at home, where she was a known and respected figure, it would probably be easier to understand.

Martha Grace's role in producing the game's most prodigious family of cricketing talent was marked by *Wisden*, who included her as the first and, until recently, with the entry of Rachael Heyhoe-Flint, the only woman in its section on the Births and Deaths of Cricketers. There she sits today, alongside her husband, three of her sons and two of her grandchildren, sons of W.G. Cricket's loss would have been immeasurable had she fallen off her father's box-kite over the Avon Gorge all those years before.

THREE

THE BOY GENIUS

The first cricket match W.G. Grace ever saw was at Bristol in 1854, when he was six. That was also the year he was first given a cricket bat of his own. The whole family turned out to watch the West Gloucestershire side, captained by his father, play a visiting All England XI led by William Clarke. He sat watching all day with his mother in a pony carriage. All he remembered in later life was that the players wore top hats.

Clarke, who built the Trent Bridge ground in Nottingham, took a group of itinerant professional cricketers around the country. Local clubs put up cash to challenge them and there was heavy betting on the outcome and much drinking among the crowd. The pros were so much better than the locals that Clarke never objected if his XI were faced by twenty-two players on the other side. Clarke had gathered around him some of the most famous players of the day, including George Parr, who took over the team when Clarke died, and feared bowlers like John Bickley, Ned Wilsher and 'Terrible Billy' Caffyn. One notable member of the team was called Julius Caesar; his slight physique and nervous disposition belied his illustrious name. He once killed a gamekeeper accidentally on a day's shooting. Bickley, a left-arm quickie from Kent, was to play a notable part in cricket history when he was no-balled in 1862 by the umpire, John Lillywhite, for bowling over-arm. This caused a national controversy that resulted in over-arm bowling being legalised by the MCC two years later. Round-arm bowling had only been accepted in 1835.

Cricket was at a crucial turning-point when W.G. began to play. The railways and the creation of new urban centres of population through industrialisation had done two things: increased mobility and created a new appetite for popular entertainment. What had been essentially a rural pastime was now to be developed as a commercial venture.

The All England XI returned to Bristol in 1855 and this time faced four of the Graces: the father and his sons Henry, E.M. and Alfred. E.M. was so small that he was given out leg before wicket to a ball that hit him in the stomach. The youngster fielded so well, however, that Clarke presented him with a bat and his mother with a copy of his cricket coaching manual. The book became a family Bible.

W.G. himself made his cricketing début for the West Gloucestershire club on the day after his ninth birthday in 1857, going in last and scoring 3 not out. He added only one run in his next two outings. But he was not deterred. 'Playing with a straight bat had become easy to me; and my uncle told me I was on the right track, and patiently I continued with it.'[1]

During the next two seasons, when he was ten and eleven, he seemed to make little progress, mainly because he lacked the physical strength to convert his solid defence into forceful scoring strokes. At the age of twelve, however, he made his first half-century for West Gloucestershire against Clifton. In the same game his father took all ten Clifton wickets and his brother E.M., now nineteen, smashed his way to 150. By this time W.G. was also being asked to bowl the occasional over. The next two seasons, however, were disappointing for him.

Then came a crisis in his life that may or may not help to explain the fact that he subsequently blossomed into a boy genius. He contracted a bad case of pneumonia which, in those days before antibiotics, was a serious threat to his life. He always insisted, despite evidence to the contrary, that the illness deprived him of the use of one lung. He was treated by his father and his elder brother Henry and nursed lovingly by his sisters. By this time he had left Rudgway School in Bristol and was being tutored at home by his brother-in-law, the Revd John Dann. His recovery was slow, but it was followed by an astonishing growth surge. He shot up to over six feet, a gigantic height for that time, towering over the entire family. His strength grew in proportion, so much so that in a piece of family horseplay he carried his elder brother, Henry, who was now thirty, and dumped him in a heap. He was a full six inches taller than E.M. His hands and feet were huge, causing wonderment to a boot boy who found he could place his fingers in the toe of W.G.'s shoe and his elbow in the heel. His hands, described as being 'like an old coal box',[2] delivered a bear-grip handshake that people soon learned to avoid.

The effect on his cricket was immediate. Although he was still only fifteen, he scored two half-centuries in club games, with a highest score of 86, enough to earn him selection for a Bristol and District side against the All England tourists, newly returned from Australia. His new strength had improved his bowling, which was almost as well regarded as his batting. Going in at number ten, he scored 32 patient runs against some of the best bowling in England and took his first wicket in top-class cricket, helped by a magnificent tumbling catch in the outfield by E.M. The makeshift Bristol team beat the All England XI for the first time, a sign of the improved standard of West Country cricket, largely inspired by Dr Grace and his remarkable family.

The All England XI were clearly impressed by the young Gilbert Grace and invited him to play for them, a great honour for a boy who was not yet sixteen. Although he was run out for 15, he watched in awe from the other end as the legendary Lillywhite scored what was decribed as 'a nonchalant century'.[3]

Ten days later, W.G. was invited to London to join a South Wales team, in place of E.M., who was away on an overseas tour. In the first game he scored 5 and 38 against Surrey at the Oval. The captain, J. Lloyd, wanted him to make way for a more experienced player in the next game against the Gentlemen of Sussex at Hove. The Graces would have none of it, however, and Mr Lloyd was soon left with egg on his face as W.G. scored 170 not out in the first innings and 56 not out in the second. His arrival on the national stage was marked by the award of a bat by the Gentlemen of Sussex, which he treasured all his life.

Only six days later came his first visit to Lord's, the esteemed headquarters of English cricket. The pitch at Lord's, however, did not live up to the ground's reputation, being pitted and covered in small stones. It was so bad that several teams, Surrey and Sussex included, refused to play on it because of the danger. W.G. batted at number three, itself a mark of his improved standing, and scored 50, despite not knowing from ball to ball whether he would face a shooter or a delivery that would lift nastily off the stony surface.

By the season of 1865, W.G. and E.M. were great rivals. The two of them beat a United England XI at Lansdown virtually on their own, sharing the wickets while the older brother hit 121, including a huge six into the River Avon.

W.G.'s bowling continued to improve; a contemporary recalled him as 'a long lanky boy who bowled very straight with a good natural leg curl'.[4]

Representing the Gentlemen of the South against the Players of the South, he took 5 wickets for 44 in the first innings and 8 for 40 in the second. This performance earned him selection for the full Gentleman v. Players match, a series he came to dominate over the next forty years, making his last appearance in 1906 at the age of fifty-eight, scoring over 6,000 runs, including 15 centuries, and taking 276 wickets.

In the two matches that summer he played solidly with both bat and ball without producing the explosive performances of E.M., who was in cracking form. Before W.G. appeared on the scene, the Players had won eighteen successive matches in the series. The tide turned with his second appearance, when the Gentlemen won at Lord's.

A contemporary account of W.G. by Lord Cobham describes him as 'a tall, loose-limbed lean boy, with some appearance of delicacy and, in marked contrast with his brother E.M., quiet and shy in manner'. At the same time his bowling style is captured thus:

His arm was as high as his shoulder . . . and while his delivery was a nice one, his action was different to what it was in his later days; it was more slinging and his pace was fast medium. He had not then acquired any of his subsequent craftiness with the ball. He used to bowl straight on the wicket, trusting to the ground to do the rest.[5]

He had clearly advanced in 1865, especially with his bowling, marked by his selection for England v. Surrey at the Oval in the last major fixture of the season, though he was disappointed not to score a first-class century. By the following year, after hunting, fishing, shooting and a great deal of walking over the winter, he had put on more weight to fill out his lean frame. He scored three club centuries at the start of the 1866 season and took 9 wickets to help the Gentlemen beat the Players at the Oval.

It was his bowling, rather than his indifferent form with the bat, that got him chosen for the England v. Surrey fixture at the Oval at the end of July, soon after his seventeenth birthday. That was the game that conclusively established his greatness: he scored 224, his first double century and at that time the highest innings ever played at the Oval. Because there were no boundaries, all those runs were literally run, a tribute to his tremendous physical fitness. This was demonstrated again on the following day, when he was given time off from fielding (an incredible thing to modern eyes) to compete in the National Olympian Association meeting at Crystal Palace. He won the 440 yards hurdles in 70 seconds, which was regarded as a very fast time. His best time at 100 yards was 10.45 seconds (pretty quick even today) and 52.15 for 400 yards. He also threw the cricket ball 122 yards in an event that was popular in those days and survived in athletics competitions until the Second World War.

He and E.M. competed in a number of athletics events that summer in Bristol, Cheltenham and London, winning many prizes. E.M. could usually just beat him in the short sprint, but the much taller W.G. was his superior over the longer distances, the jumps and the hurdles. In 1869, his last full season in athletics, he was first in seventeen events and second in nine.

It goes without saying, of course, that his athletics career preceded his famous gargantuan girth. In fact, the pictorial records of W.G., most of which were taken in his later years when he was a national institution and the craft of photography had developed, give a false impression of his physical appearance. By then he must have weighed at least 18 stones. In his prime as a player he was around 12 stones. The few pictures of his golden decade, 1868–78, show a lithe athlete in the peak of condition, with a competitive glare in the eye that was frequently noted.

Although he was later jeered in the field because he could not get down to the ball – 'the ground has moved too far away',[6] he said sadly – he had earlier succeeded his brother E.M. as the best fielder in the country at point or cover-point. During his career those bucket-like hands held no fewer than 875 catches.

His double century at the Oval in 1866 was followed in August by another brilliant innings of 173 not out for the Gentlemen of the South, a knock judged by many observers to have been even better. 'A finer innings could not be witnessed', said *The Times*.[7] He also took 7 for 92 in the first innings. He scored over 2,000 runs that season at an average of 54. He was now, at the age of eighteen, the leading batsman in England and one of the most successful bowlers as well.

The next season, 1867, should have seen a full flowering of his young genius. It was not to be, however, mainly because he suffered injuries to his ankle and hand and had a debilitating bout of scarlet fever that put him out of action for six weeks. He scored no centuries that season, but had a good year with the ball, taking 39 wickets at only 7 runs apiece. He took part in two farcical matches at Lord's for the Gentlemen against the Players, in both of which 30 wickets fell on the first day. The pitch was described by *The Times* as 'a kind of tessellated, lumpy sward, where patches of rusty yellow strive with faded green'.[8] If the surface made batting impossible, it was none the less popular with the bowlers. W.G. took 17 wickets in the two games, helped by four stunning catches at point by E.M.

He took 44 wickets at an average of 16 and scored three first-class centuries in the hot summer of 1868. The best was at Lord's, again for the Gentlemen, hitting 134 out of a total of 193. He later regarded it as one of his best innings, chiefly because he had to master the unruly Lord's pitch. *The Times* described it as 'one of the finest' innings of the season. He also took 10 wickets in the match to help the Gentlemen to another victory.

His other two centuries that season came at Canterbury for the South of the Thames against the North and was the first time anyone had ever scored two hundreds in the same match. W.G. welcomed the fact that at Canterbury there were marked boundaries, which saved him running for everything.

That same season Gloucestershire appeared as a county side for the first time, beating the Middlesex club and ground side at Lord's with three Graces to the fore (E.M., W.G. and G.F., who at the age of nineteen was developing into a promising young batsman). They played their first inter-county match the following year.

W.G. received an unexpected twenty-first birthday present that year – membership of the MCC. The club had spotted his talent early and recognised the power of his popular appeal. But there was calculation in their gesture too. Had Grace chosen to throw in his lot with the itinerant professionals, MCC might have soon lost control of the game. The MCC secretary, Robert Fitzgerald, a genial, easy-going character with a beard even longer than W.G.'s, had always acknowledged the young Grace's genius and the power he had to influence the course of the game. It was he who backed W.G. for MCC membership, even though his rustic, non-public school background, emphasised by a slight West Country burr, was not the normal social milieu from which the club then recruited its members.

Although W.G. did, in fact, go on to lead his own itinerant team, the United South XI, he would never countenance a break with the governing body of cricket, as the northern professionals wanted to do. A serious rift developed between the north and south, matching the one that was to divide rugby league and rugby union for over a century. It was eventually closed by the new county championship, to which Grace was committed through his family link with Gloucestershire. More counties were formed and started playing each other on a regular basis during the 1870s.

For Grace's United South tours, clubs would offer him a lump sum to appear. He would pay his players as little as he could get away with, usually £5, and keep the rest for himself after paying expenses. It was his main source of income before he qualified as a doctor in 1879. One vignette of this time is very suggestive – an old man recalled W.G. standing under the shade of a tree in the outfield arguing over expenses with the local secretary. It seems remarkable that he managed to retain his amateur status throughout this period as a mercenary. The explanation seems to be that his standing was of such mythic proportions, and his drawing power so self-evident, that questions were simply not asked of him.

The public had begun to expect new miracles every time he went out to bat and he continued to provide them. He scored a century on his début for MCC against Oxford University and three more against Surrey, Nottinghamshire and Kent, totalling six in the season as a whole. His 121 against Nottinghamshire won him a wager that he could top the score of the great batsman, Richard Daft, who had got 103. On a rare trip north to Sheffield he scored a brilliant 122 and took 6 for 57 with the ball.

An innings of 180 for the Gentlemen of the South at the Oval brought a tribute from the *Daily Telegraph* that is worth quoting for the graphic account it gives of the Champion, as he was now universally known, in full flow:

He has made even larger scores than the 180, but we doubt whether a better innings has ever been played by a cricketer past or present. The characteristic of Mr Grace's play was that he knew exactly where every ball he hit would go. Just the strength required was expended and no more. When the fieldsmen were placed injudiciously too deep, he would quietly send a ball half-way towards them with a gentle tap and content himself with a modest single. If they came in a little nearer, the shoulders opened out and the powerful arms swung round as he lashed at the first loose ball and sent it away through the crowded ring of visitors until one heard a big thump as it struck against the farthest fence. Watching most other men – even good players – your main object is to see how they will defend themselves against the bowling; watching Mr Gilbert Grace, you can hardly help feeling as though the batsman himself were the assailant.[9]

No wonder *Lillywhite's Annual* concluded its summary of 1869 by saying that W.G. was 'generally admitted to be the most wonderful cricketer that ever handled a bat'.[10] By 1866 he was acknowledged as the best batsman in the country: three years later, when he was still only twenty-one, he was being described as the best who had ever played. The boy genius was a boy no longer.

THE GOLDEN YEARS, 1870–7

By 1870 the cricket season was developing a more formal structure. Until then matches had been fairly haphazard, the same players often appearing in different guises for different teams, usually attracted by the money on offer. Annual fixtures were simply repeated. The development of the railways and tarmacadam roads made it possible for clubs to be more ambitious with their fixture list, moving away from their immediate locality.

The county structure, guided by the MCC, started to take form a year later. Gloucestershire, inspired by Dr Grace snr, with E.M. as secretary, played its first inter-county match in 1870. This was against Surrey and took place, appropriately, on Durdham Down, where the old Dr Grace used to practise from 6 a.m. before starting his medical rounds. There was a band playing and a large crowd roared the home county to victory in their first match. W.G. took 9 wickets and young Fred 7.

In the return match at the Oval W.G. scored the county's first century, 143. Then Gloucestershire beat MCC by an innings at Lord's, thanks to an inspired knock of 172 by the Champion, played on a wet pitch in bad light, and described as 'one of the grandest innings ever'.[1] The press were euphoric. According to the *Sportsman*, the innings included 'some of the finest hitting and brilliant batting under most disadvantageous conditions of ground and light that has [sic] ever been seen in any match'.[2] Such praise created a new audience for the game and people came from far and wide to see the Champion in action. It was at this time that signs first began to be seen: 'Threepence for entry, Sixpence if W.G. Grace is playing'.

Even that, though, was not to be his greatest innings of 1870, for he scored 215 against the Players at the Oval in a display which, according to the *Daily Telegraph*, 'never was surpassed'.[3] Some purists would dispute this, however, citing a 66 he scored against Yorkshire on the dreaded Lord's pitch against ferocious bowling by George Freeman. C.E. Green, his batting partner, said: 'We were both cruelly battered about.'[4] Freeman himself wrote later: 'It was a marvel the doctor was not either maimed or unnerved for the rest of his days or killed outright.'[5] W.G. scored over 3,000 runs in that glorious summer.

The next season, 1871, he recorded the finest statistics of his career: 3,696 runs, ten centuries, two of them double hundreds, and an average of 78. The measure of his superiority over all other players – a superiority not matched until Don Bradman in the next century – is that the next highest batting average was less than half. It was Fred, with 34.

What distinguished W.G.'s batting was his immaculate placing of the ball. He was assisted in this by the fact that the quality of grounds was improving all the time; even Lord's was dug up three years later. Experts noticed that, through his exceptional timing, Grace could score runs off balls that other players would be happy to defend. Even when he was fending off a shooter – he was once cheered to the echo by a discriminating Lord's crowd for keeping out four in succession – he learned to twist the bat so that the ball would squirt away for runs. Another feature was his determination to redeem any failure in the first innings by succeeding in the second. For example, in one match that year, a benefit played for H.H. Stephenson, the man who captained the first England tour of Australia, he was given out lbw first ball. It was evidently a doubtful decision and the great man showed his displeasure. In the second innings he made up for it with 268 runs, many the result of fierce, even vindictive hitting.

The same thing happened at a benefit for John Lillywhite at Hove. W.G. was bowled first ball after arriving late at the ground and missing out on net practice, something he never allowed to happen again. His dismissal was bad news for the beneficiary, who counted on the doctor's presence to draw in the crowds. Again W.G. made up for his lapse with 217 in the second innings.

Despite these two double centuries, there was still a dispute in 1871, as in previous seasons, as to which was his greatest innings. Grace himself thought it was an innings of 189 not out on a rain-affected wicket at Lord's. Others recalled a magnificent 178, also at Lord's, before a bank holiday crowd so big and hard to control that turnstiles had to be introduced for the following season.

The centuries flowed on – at Lord's, the Oval, Canterbury, and on his first appearance at Fenner's against Cambridge University. There had been some talk of W.G. going up to Cambridge, but he stuck with his medical studies at Bristol. It was also not clear that his father could really afford it. By now he was a novel star attraction whenever he ventured beyond the West Country or London. Everybody wanted to see the Champion and, just as important perhaps, to *say* they had seen him.

The *Sporting Gazette* reported:

> It was chiefly the prospect of beholding the great batsman perform which drew together these enormous crowds and therefore swelled the exchequer of the county club.[6]

At Nottingham he emptied the factories, attracting a crowd of 10,000 on the first day and 12,000 on the second. The pressure to succeed was immense, to avoid disappointing his fans. He scored 79 in the first innings, then having been told by Daft that nobody had yet scored a century on the ground, proceeded to get one in the second innings. At the Canterbury Festival in August 1871 he was run out for 40 in a close decision that annoyed the crowd, who showed their displeasure by booing. The fact that the crowd wanted to see Grace batting increased the pressure on umpires to give him the benefit of any doubt, because, as he is reported to have said to one of them: 'The crowd have come to see me bat, not to see you umpire.'

Whenever he failed, which was rarely these days, it was against the laws of nature. As the *Daily Telegraph* noted, 'imagine Patti singing outrageously out of tune; imagine Mr Gladstone violating all the rules of grammar'.[7] At the end of his best season so far, *Lillywhite's Companion* noted that 'his defence has been more stubborn, his hitting more brilliant and his timing and placing of the ball more judicious and skilful than during the previous summer'.[8]

The year ended sadly, however, with the death of Dr Grace snr at Christmas. Although his son had many glorious days to come on the cricket field, at least Henry Mills Grace had lived long enough to see him in full flower.

The start of the 1872 season was badly affected by rain, against which the grounds had no protection. One writer said at the time: 'Mr W.G. Grace cares rather less for the rain than a young sheldrake.'[9] In one ridiculous rain-affected game at Lord's the MCC team, including Grace, were bowled out for 16.

Generally, though, because of Grace's exploits, the belief gained ground that the bat had too much superiority over the ball and attempts were made to redress the balance. Four stumps were tried and the three stumps were made higher and wider. The experiment was soon abandoned, however.

At Lord's that year W.G. made 170 not out in 225 minutes, an innings rated by the *Sportsman* as being 'as superfine and irreproachable a display of batting as he has ever shown in his career'.[10] The crowd ran onto the pitch and chased him to the dressing-room. His travels away from the capital opened his doctor's eyes to the disparity between rich and poor and the blighting effects of industrialisation on the environment and people's health. When he scored 150 at Bramall Lane in Sheffield he found that his flannels were stained by the soot from the nearby factories. He hit two balls out of the ground, prompting a local to say: 'He dab 'em but seldom, and when he do dab 'em he dab 'em for foor.'[11] He then went further north, taking a team up to Scotland. They were dismissed in the first innings for 49, much to the disappointment of the Glaswegians. As usual, however, Grace made it up to them in the second innings with a score of 114, including six mighty sixes. An unfortunate woman in the crowd was hit on the arm by one of them and, despite moving for safety, was later hit on the chest by another. One of the players, asked to comment on Grace's display, said: 'The ground wasn't big enough today.'[12]

By now neither Scotland, nor even the United Kingdom, was big enough to contain the great man's fame as it spread outwards to the Commonwealth and wherever cricket was played. It was time for W.G. to appear on an even wider stage. He was to go on three overseas tours (described in Chapter 6, A Travelling Man). He toured Canada and the United States with an MCC team in 1872/3 and spent the following winter in Australia, returning there twenty years later. For all the mishaps and misadventures of touring in those days, Australia was to recharge Grace's batteries, offering him new challenges. Having effectively mastered bowling attacks at home, he found the Australians forced him to learn new tricks. This had the effect of rekindling his interest in the game at times when he might have been tempted to retire to his family and his West Country medical practice.

In 1873, at the age of twenty-five, he took a wife, Agnes Nicholls Day, the daughter of his first cousin. She was a quiet, dark-haired girl who lived with her parents at Clapham Common. They were married in London at a ceremony conducted by his brother-in-law and former tutor, the Revd Dann.

Some historians have noted that Grace decided to marry soon after his return from the tour to Canada and the United States, speculating that his mind may have been bent towards matrimony by the sight of the many young ladies who had flocked to meet the tourists and often danced the night away with them. Grace himself was reported to be as sure-footed on the dance floor as he was at the crease. Although some of the touring party were as energetic at wenching and carousing as their successors a century later, W.G.'s somewhat austere personal reputation remained intact.

The season of 1873, along with those of 1871, 1876 and his *annus mirabilis*, 1895, was among the finest of his career. He scored over 2,000 runs at an average of 71 (his highest ever in a season), including six first-class centuries and took over a hundred wickets, thereby recording the 'double' for the first time in cricket history. But it was not just the achievements themselves that were so remarkable; it was also the distance he put between himself and everyone else in the game. He scored four hundreds for the Gentlemen, his highest score of the season being 192 not out for the South v. the North at the Oval. He scored a memorable 145 at Prince's, a ground in Hans Place, Knightsbridge, that has long since made way for luxury apartments. This attracted thousands of curious new spectators from the West End of London.

By now the suggestion had re-emerged that he was spoiling the game and that the rules might have to be changed to make the contest more equal. *The Times* suggested that he might have to be blindfolded or play with one hand behind his back. The *Sporting Gazette* wrote: 'What is to be done with him? He is really ruining the cricket in first-class matches. He demoralises the fielders and breaks the heart of the bowlers.'[13]

It is certainly true that, once the quality of wickets started improving, Grace virtually destroyed the fast bowlers who had relied on bad pitches for their success. They were almost afraid to bowl anything within his mighty reach. He celebrated the newly laid pitch at Lord's with 163 and followed up with 158 in just over three hours at the Oval. The *Daily Telegraph* commented: 'To say Mr W.G. Grace is far and away the best batsman that ever scored a run is to tell an old tale. . . . This week Mr Grace's star has been fast rising to the zenith.'[14]

He was particularly delighted with Gloucestershire's form that season, in which they were level with Nottinghamshire in the still unofficial county championship. His own contribution was an unbeaten 160 at Clifton which included several big hits out of the ground. In a practice match for United South that year, he made a measured hit of 140 yards. Playing for them against Seventeen of Coventry, he took 25 wickets (14 and 11 in each innings) and took five catches off others' bowling, making him responsible for 30 wickets in the match. It was in this game that he ran out a batsman who left his crease to recover his belt, an incident that still rankled in the city over a century later. When he took Gloucestershire to Sheffield to play Yorkshire, there were 12,000 spectators. Counties started asking for a guarantee that he would play and were naturally put out when he had to plead another engagement.

He spent the winter of 1873/4 in Australia, but showed that he had lost none of his appetite for the game by scoring 259 in three hours, including ten sixes, for the Thornbury club, near Bristol, only four days after he got off the boat. In all he scored eleven centuries in 1874, eight of them in first-class matches, and scored 1,664 first-class runs at an average of 52. In a friendly game at Cheltenham he was made to bat with a broomstick and scored 35 runs. Fortunately, he had learned how to bat with a stick as a boy.

His bowling, meanwhile, kept on improving. In 1874 he took 139 wickets at an average of 12. This was the start of his vintage period as a bowler, in which he took 100 wickets in each of six successive seasons.

The following year, 1875, showed a relative downturn in his batting, only three centuries and an average of 32, but he achieved his best-ever bowling haul, 191 wickets. His athleticism was still highly praised. A.J. Webbe, an Oxford undergraduate who scored 203 with him in an opening partnership for the Gentlemen that summer, enthused: 'How he used to run in those days; then there was no sign of stoutness in his figure.'[15] In that game W.G. scored

152 runs out of 242 in 205 minutes, an innings described by one top-class player as 'the most titanic display of batting that I have ever seen'.[16] Even so, articles started appearing to suggest that Grace was past his best — as, indeed, they were to go on appearing for the next quarter of a century.

The people of Sheffield could not have shared that opinion, for 20,000 of them turned out to see him score 111 out of a total of 174. He and his brothers E.M. and G.F. had a hand in the fall of all Yorkshire wickets in both innings. W.G. and E.M. were later to bowl out several sides between them in club matches for Thornbury. Some judges thought his best innings of the season was 35 for MCC at Lord's against the left-arm wiles of Alfred Shaw, the best bowler of the time, who took 7 for 7 in the second innings.

By 1876, perhaps through enjoying the comforts of married life — he and Agnes now had a son, William Gilbert Grace jnr — his shape began to expand ominously towards the stereotype familiar from the later photographs. He was probably 15 stones by this time and actually rose to at least 18 stones while he was still playing. He may even have been over 20 stones when he played club cricket in retirement. None the less, he still had the energy to go on breaking records and, despite a relatively slow start in May and June, he found his best form in July. In August, as the record books show, he was to indulge in the most remarkable burst of scoring ever seen.

W.G. had recovered his best form with a cracking 169 at Lord's for the Gentlemen, including a century before lunch, and also took 9 wickets in the match. The crowd chased their hero all the way back to the pavilion. He went on to Grimsby for a challenge match that did not rank as a first-class fixture. His batting, however, was of the very highest class and he achieved the top score of his career, 400 (some say it was actually 399 and that Grace instructed the scorer to top it up). To prove that his increased weight had not reduced his legendary stamina, he batted for over thirteen hours and ran no fewer than 158 singles, a severe test for his enlarged new waistline. *Lillywhite's Annual* wrote poetically of this innings: 'No paint can add to the beauty of the lily, nor will gilding improve refined gold. To extol W.G. Grace's merits as a cricketer would be superfluous. . . . [He is] first − the rest nowhere.'[17]

To add to this magical day in his life, news arrived that Mrs Grace had given birth to their second son, Henry Edgar. As he stood toasting the new arrival in champagne, W.G. could have been forgiven for thinking he had reached the summit of his achievements on the cricket field. Incredibly, however, this was not so. After scoring 114 not out to help Richard Daft's benefit at Trent Bridge, he went on to Hull, where he hit 126 in 150 minutes. After that he went south to Canterbury, where he scored 9 and 91 for a combined Kent–Gloucestershire team, then started the run of high scores that became a legend.

Playing to save what seemed a lost cause for MCC v. Kent, he hit out to such effect in the second innings that he passed the highest score then recorded in a first-class match, 278, and went on to 344. The second day was fiercely hot, so he refreshed himself at periodic intervals with his favourite concoction, champagne and soda. The press, by now running out of superlatives, were suitably ecstatic – 'the greatest batting exhibition yet recorded', 'a stupendous achievement', 'by far the most remarkable event in the annals of cricket'.[18] Grace himself wrote afterwards: 'I risked a little more than usual, helped myself more freely than I would have done under different circumstances, and everything came off.'[19]

Two days later, back at Clifton, he scored 177 and took 8 wickets for 69 to help Gloucestershire beat their great rivals, Nottinghamshire. His innings included a six into the grandstand which was caught flamboyantly by his brother Fred, who was surrounded by admiring young ladies. To add to the fun, W.G. amused the crowd by pretending to walk off.

It was then Yorkshire's turn at the Cheltenham College ground, which W.G. said was the best pitch he had ever played on. He carried his bat for another triple century, 318 not out. He was so commanding in this innings that the Yorkshire bowlers did not want to bowl to him and fell out with each other in the field.

In that vintage spell – never repeated in the history of cricket – Grace had scored 839 runs in eight days, 1,164 runs in 16 days, and 1,389 runs in the month of August alone, more than any other batsman scored in the whole season. His total for the year, including the relatively fallow months of May and June, was 2,622 runs at an average of 62. He also took 139 first-class wickets at 18.9.

No one, not even the Champion, could cap that astonishing performance, and his 1877 season seemed flat in comparison, even though he was still the leading batsman in England with 1,474 runs at an average of just under 40. His best innings was 261 for the South v. the North at Hans Place, one of the last games to be played on the Knightsbridge ground before builders got hold of the site. At one point in this innings Grace's score stood at 202 out of a total of 300. He is better remembered for his bowling that season, taking 179 wickets at an average of 12, the second best haul of his long career. It included his best-ever performance, 9 for 55 and 8 for 34 for Gloucestershire against Nottinghamshire. In the second innings he took 7 wickets in 17 balls for no runs, including 3 wickets in one over. Other match-winning figures that season were 8 for 36 and 6 for 19.

His increased girth did not appear to have affected his success with the ball, though he now delivered it more slowly and relied on tricking the batsman out. One of his favourite ploys was to tempt the batsman to hit an apparently bad ball on the leg-side straight down the throat of one of his two long-legs. Brother Fred was usually one of these sentinels stalking the boundary.

W.G. (1848–1915) in full flow, a study in balance and power.
Courtesy of Gloucestershire County Cricket Club (GCCC)

Dr Henry Mills Grace, W.G.'s father, a fine horseman who sired five doctors. (GCCC)

Mother Martha Grace: a county match was abandoned out of respect when she died. (GCCC)

The Chesnuts, near Bristol, where the Graces lived for many years and laid out a pitch in the grounds. (GCCC)

W.G. in his prime at the age of twenty-two, a lithe athlete before he put on weight.
(GCCC)

West Gloucestershire, the nucleus of the future county team, in 1866. Eight are members of
the Grace family. Back row, left to right: Revd H.W. Barber, Dr H.M. Grace, H. Grunning,
Alfred Pocock (Grace's uncle and coach). Middle: W.G. Grace (aged eighteen), Henry Grace,
E.M. Grace, Alfred Grace. Front: F. Baker, W.J. Pocock, G.F. Grace, R. Brotherhood.
(GCCC)

Gloucestershire CCC, 1877. Back row, left to right: W.O. Mobberly, W. Fairbanks,
G.F. Grace (holding ball), F.G. Monkland, W.R. Gilbert, W. Midwinter, C.K. Pullin
(umpire). Front row: Capt. Kingscote, F. Townsend, R.F. Miles, W.G. Grace (with bat),
E.M. Grace. (GCCC)

E.M. Grace, W.G.'s elder brother, known as 'the Coroner', a hard-hitting, unorthodox batsman who was said to be 'overflowing with cricket at every pore, full of lusty life'. He was secretary of Gloucestershire for thirty-nine years. (GCCC)

G.F. (Fred) Grace, the youngest and most attractive of the brothers, who died tragically at the age of twenty-nine after playing in his first Test for England in 1880. (GCCC)

E.M. and W.G. The rivalry with his elder brother, which was displayed on the athletics track as well as the cricket field, was a spur to W.G.'s ambition in his youth. (GCCC)

W.G.'s round-arm tweaker in middle age. In his youth he had bowled much quicker. He took 2,876 first-class wickets in his career, including 100 wickets in a season seven times.
(The Beldam Collection)

W.G. depicted in an advertisement. Even though he was nominally an amateur, W.G. made a good living from the game. (The Robert Opie Collection)

One of the last pictures of Grace in old age. (GCCC)

The Grace Gates at Lord's, opened in 1923, dedicated to 'the Great Cricketer'. (GCCC)

Gloucestershire were unofficial county champions that season and demonstrated their class with a victory over a strong England XI. The county game was now becoming more popular, drawing its own loyal supporters, and the itinerant circus teams soon became a thing of the past.

That season, 1877, ended Grace's so-called golden period, though he still had one superlative season some years ahead of him. It was time to attend to his medical studies and to end his protracted apprenticeship to the family profession. Before doing that, however, he needed some medical attention himself when he nearly lost an eye in a shooting accident on Lord Westmorland's estate in Northamptonshire. Had that incident ended his career, it would still have been the most remarkable in the history of cricket. He had already changed the game beyond recognition. And he was still, though it is hard to believe, under thirty years of age.

DOCTOR
AT LAST

Although the appellation 'Dr' is part of the abiding Grace legend, he had played his greatest cricket for more than a decade before he became entitled to use it in 1879. He then practised medicine for only twenty years before abruptly quitting the profession at the age of fifty-one.

It seems extraordinary that Dr Henry Mills Grace should have persuaded all five of his sons to follow a medical career, for there was no previous record of doctors in the family. It may have been partly for economic reasons, so that he – and later his eldest son Henry – could help to teach the others, passing on the textbooks in the way some families pass down clothing.

All of them practised in the Bristol area. Henry, the most serious doctor in the family, had a practice at Kingswood Hill; E.M. at Thornbury, where he was the Coroner (which became his nickname on the cricket field); and Alfred at Chipping Sodbury, where he was famed for his daring riding and boxing rather than for cricket. All the brothers took on public medical appointments, ministering to the local workhouse, lunatic asylum, the Army or the mines.

W.G. enrolled as a 'perpetual student' at the Bristol Medical School in 1868. The word proved appropriate, for he did not qualify as a doctor for another eleven years. The training of doctors was casual and chaotic and there was not even a medical register until 1858. There were three kinds of medical men (no women, of course): apothecaries, surgeons and physicians. Physicians were the thinkers and researchers into medicine who diagnosed diseases and proposed remedies. The apothecaries mixed and supplied the medicines, much as a pharmacist would do today. Surgeons did the practical stuff, like setting fractures, lancing boils and carrying out primitive amputations.

By the second half of the nineteenth century there were three ways of qualifying as a doctor. A small number of men did so by virtue of a degree at Oxford, Cambridge or some Scottish universities. In London, dominated for centuries by the guild system, you had to become a licentiate of the London College. Most aspirant doctors, like the Graces, registered as apprentices, later called medical students, at one of the twelve teaching hospitals in London or at one of nine in the provinces. Eventually, after periods of academic study and clinical experience, the students were able to sit for professional diplomas offered by the Colleges of Surgeons and Physicians in London and Edinburgh, or by the Society of Apothecaries.

The Grace family, including the father, studied locally at first and then attended various London medical schools because the Bristol Medical School, attached to Bristol Royal Infirmary, was not then empowered to award degrees. When Grace enrolled at Bristol in 1868, he must have cut a curious figure. As a history of the hospital put it later, 'he was in his twenty-first year and was already one of the most famous men in England'.[1] The doctors would still have worn silk top hats, but the custom had died out by the time he qualified.

Grace was a pupil of Mr Robert Tibbitts, a surgeon and a quirky character known as 'Slasher' to the students, who was only five years older than Grace. Tibbitts was a stickler for cleanliness at a time when standards were very slack. One surgeon at the hospital kept the needles he used for stitching up patients in the curtains, so that he knew where they were. Others kept them in the waistband of their trousers. Operations were often performed in ordinary clothes. Although Tibbitts was to die at thirty-seven, he was instrumental in reforming the Medical School and merging it with Bristol University.

The hospital's history refers intriguingly to a burly, bearded student who 'represented a terrific aspect in the operation room, with saws, forceps and knives stuck into his belt, looking very much like a comic bandit'.[2] It is tempting, but probably wrong (since he would have been well enough known to be identified by the writer), to think of this bandit as W.G.

In 1872 Grace became a physician's pupil under Dr Frederick Britan. The school was then grossly inefficient, with rowdy classes often supervised by a porter. It is no wonder it took him so long to qualify. The following year Grace enrolled at St Bartholomew's Hospital in London, moving from the West Country with his new wife to Earls Court and later to Acton. Among his teachers at Barts were Mr A.E. Cumberbatch, who taught anatomy, Mr (later Professor) Howard Marsh, general surgery, and Dr Samuel Gee, a distinguished diagnostician.

This was the heart of Grace's golden period as a player and his medical studies clearly took second place. It seems unlikely that he took his textbooks into the dressing-room or read them on the balcony in those rare periods when he was not on the field. He was always dismissive of players who read books, arguing that it damaged their eyesight for play. It is not perhaps surprising that his friends and family began to despair of him ever qualifying. In 1876, after a family discussion, he moved to the Westminster Hospital, where he was supervised by Dr W.H. Allchin, who lectured on physiology and pathology. Finally, in 1879, he knuckled down to a concentrated period of study, coached by Professor Marsh from Bart's, and assisted by a wet summer that cancelled much of the cricket programme. As a result, he managed to put together an unusual hybrid qualification, MRCS (Member of the Royal College of Physicians) in London and LRCP (Licentiate of the Royal College of Physicians) in Edinburgh. It was said that his Scottish examiner, Dr Charles Bell, 'must have felt an enormous weight on his shoulders when this huge bearded celebrity sat down across the table in the examination hall'.[3] There was certainly much relief in the Grace family when he passed, though his father had not lived to see him qualify.

Grace was far from being an impoverished medical student. In the summer of 1879 he had received £1,458 (rounded up to £1,500 by Lord Russell) from a benefit match put on for him by the MCC at Lord's and the cheque enabled him to buy a practice in Stapleton Road, an unfashionable area of Bristol. He was also given a clock and obelisks made of marble and bronze.

Although he retained the surgery, he and Agnes moved their domestic quarters as their family grew, first to Thrissel House nearby, then to Victoria Square in Clifton (from where he walked several miles to work each day to keep up his fitness) and finally to Ashley Grange, which had a garden big enough to allow the whole Gloucestershire team to practise in it. For the next twenty years he doctored in the winter and played cricket in the summer, using a locum to look after his Bristol practice, for which Gloucestershire paid him a special sum of £20, later raised in stages to £36.

For the four seasons after he qualified, he played in fewer matches as he set about establishing his medical practice and scored less than 1,000 runs in each of them. There were rumours that he would soon give up cricket to concentrate on medicine and there were times when he was tempted to do so.

He was surgeon, medical officer and public vaccinator to the Barton Hill district of Bristol. At that time much of a doctor's life was devoted to attending patients, often children, suffering from tuberculosis, diarrhoea, measles, whooping cough, scarlet fever and diphtheria. In 1875, 408 people had died in the Bristol area in a scarlet fever epidemic. W. G.'s only daughter, Bessie, was to die of typhoid in 1899. Without antibiotics, there was little doctors could do for their patients, apart from isolate them and keep them warm and clean, applying common sense and a friendly bedside manner.

Grace was no scholar and there is no evidence that he was a naturally gifted healer, but there are many reports of him bringing comfort to the sick and injured through the sheer force of his personality and the glamour of his celebrity. One case involved five miners who were badly burnt in an accident at Pennymills. They visibly cheered up when he arrived and, because he had a regular surgery at the pit, knew them all by name. He once took a boat to reach a patient when the roads were flooded and in another recorded case he was appalled at the poverty he found in a slum home and gave a little boy half a crown. The mother thought he had made a mistake, expecting a penny, and sent the boy to Grace's surgery to return it. He gave them another half-crown as a reward for their honesty and helped the father to find a job.

One night he and Agnes were disturbed by a man shouting up at their bedroom that his wife was ill again. The bearded doctor put his head out and called: 'Warm half a pint of old beer and give her that. I'll see her in the morning. She'll be all right.'[4] A chimney-sweep turned up at the surgery one day and asked for a tonic. 'You want exercise, not medicine,' said Grace and called to a maid: 'Throw down those boxing gloves.' The sweep ran out into the street, fearing for his life.[5] One unsupported story is that he tired of tending to the injuries a woman suffered at the hands of her husband and tore down the street in a rage and hammered at the door. When the man opened it, W.G. is said to have punched him on the nose and warned him to expect the same treatment if he ever hit his wife again.

His medical credentials were sometimes required on the cricket field. In 1887 there was a gruesome case when one of his Gloucestershire team, A.C.M. Croome, tore his neck on some iron railings at Old Trafford. Grace held the wound together with his hands for half an hour, preventing the man bleeding to death, before the gash could be stitched. A Kent player, C.J.M. Fox, dislocated his shoulder against Gloucestershire. While E.M., who was also playing, held the player down, W.G. manipulated the joint back into place. In another Kent game he stitched a cut eye for the opposing wicket-keeper, Richard Palmer, and later claimed to be affronted when he was stumped by his ungrateful patient. 'After all I've done for you,' he growled, 'that's what you do to me.'[6]

His medical career ended abruptly in 1899 in circumstances that have never been fully explained. Later he told the writer Bernard Darwin, while playing golf with him, that it had been caused by the shifting of parish boundaries which had affected several medical practices in the area. This happened to coincide with an offer he received to become player-manager of the newly-formed London County Cricket Club at Crystal Palace. Since his relations were already soured with Gloucestershire, he decided that this was too good an offer to refuse. So he and his wife, with their two youngest children, upped sticks from his beloved West Country for south London. For him it was another adventure; for Agnes it was going home.

The doctor may have hung up his stethoscope at the age of fifty-one, but many more years were to pass before he was ready to hang up his bat.

A TRAVELLING
MAN

I t was Robert Fitzgerald, the affable MCC
secretary, who encouraged Grace to take part in a
tour of Canada and the United States at the end of
the 1872 season. Indeed, the Canadians, who offered
to pay for the tour, stipulated that the great man had
to be included or the deal was off. Their aim was to
encourage cricket in Canada, which had not taken off
in the way it had in Australia, partly because of the
competing attraction of baseball and partly because
of the strong French influence in the country.

Fitzgerald had problems finding enough so-called
amateurs ready to undertake a long and possibly
arduous tour in unknown terrain and finally set off
from Liverpool with only twelve players (one of
whom broke a finger fielding to Grace in the first
practice session when they landed in Quebec). They
included the future Lord Harris and A.N. 'Monkey'

Hornby, of Lancashire, who was to open many times with Grace and was the man who abandoned a county match against Gloucestershire when news of Martha Grace's death reached Old Trafford.

Grace was horribly sea-sick on the nine-day voyage but recovered in time to enjoy the whales and icebergs off Newfoundland. The ship, the SS *Sarmantian*, also contained 200 waifs and strays from the London streets who were being offered a new life in the New World.

The arrangements for the tour were chaotic, with trains missed, hotels unbooked and most of the grounds unfit for serious cricket. Another player was struck on the head while practising on a deadly pitch, bringing the team down to ten men, who still turned out to be more than enough for their weak opposition.

Four things saved the tour from disaster: the generous hospitality of the hosts, who laid on lavish balls and banquets; the chance to enjoy country pursuits like shooting and fishing in a magnificent setting (Grace, great countryman that he was, lapped it all up); W.G.'s outstanding form with the bat, which provoked wonder wherever they went; and Fitzgerald's hearty diplomacy.

The tourists seem to have been followed by dozens of beautiful women. These are coyly mentioned in all the contemporary accounts, in Toronto, Ottowa and Montreal – Canadian young men evidently being, in Fitzgerald's phrase, 'too busy for matters of the heart'. There seems to have been no shortage of champagne or other liquors and there is more than one reference to players missing trains or being late for matches because of hangovers. In New York an American journalist wrote: 'John Bull's sons are generally fond of good cheer. They have a strange proclivity for taking their ease at an inn.'[1] Given the natural reticence of the time, we may take it from this that they were frequently plastered.

It seems incredible that Englishmen should have played cricket in the heart of New York, at Hoboken, over 125 years ago. The best of the local players were imported from baseball and W.G. admired their skills in the field. The admiration was mutual, as the Americans, 2,000 of whom turned out to watch in New York, marvelled at Grace's 'splendid physique and easy exercise of muscle'. He was lionised at post-match banquets and one speaker said he 'must be known to more people by sight to more people in England than Mr Gladstone himself'.[2] Bands struck up 'Rule Britannia' or 'God Save the Queen' wherever Grace and his colleagues appeared. He was forced into after-dinner speaking on this tour, but never enjoyed it, using the same formula for every speech, with slight amendments to suit the local audience. His voice was high and rather fluty for his massive bulk.

Fitzgerald concluded: 'Victory is of course largely due to the never-failing bat of W.G. Grace.'[3] But he doubted whether cricket would ever replace baseball in the US. 'No Canadian,' he added, 'is likely to become a second W.G. if he lives to be a hundred and plays till past four score.'[4]

Grace was offered a gift of two bear cubs to bring home, but wisely declined. Agnes, whom he married soon after his return, might not have been best pleased. The next tour, to Australia and New Zealand the following winter, was to be their honeymoon. The invitation had come to W.G. himself from the Melbourne Cricket Club, asking him to put a touring side together. The fee he demanded in reply, £1,500, staggered them at first, but they finally raised the money by joining forces with two other Melbourne clubs. The other players were to get £170 each, itself a mark of the Champion's pulling power and the disparity between him and other cricketers of the day. Many of the leading professionals, including Alfred Shaw and Tom Emmett, were not tempted by this bait, but he made up a party of twelve, including his brother Fred and cousin W.R. Gilbert, plus Henry Jupp, James Lillywhite and Arthur Bush, the Gloucestershire wicket-keeper, who had been Grace's best man at his wedding.

There were five amateurs and seven professionals in the party, which soon caused bad blood between the two groups. It was not to be a happy tour. It almost started in disaster, when Jupp, nursing the mother and father of all hangovers, missed the boat and had to be taken aboard on a tugboat carrying the mail. After enduring a storm that caused sea-sickness in the Bay of Biscay, the team stopped at Malta and at the newly opened Suez Canal, which failed to impress them. Grace nearly killed one of his team while boxing on board to break the monotony. It finally took them forty-six days to reach Australia, via Ceylon (now Sri Lanka). When they arrived in Melbourne to see a game of cricket between local clubs, they were astonished to see the crowd invade the pitch because they disagreed with an umpire's decision. It was their first taste of the passion that Australians brought to their sport.

W.G. was not impressed by the standards of pitch preparation in Australia and had to bully the Melbourne ground staff into using the roller. He had constant battles with opposing captains throughout the tour about the quality of the pitches and when they should be rolled.

In the nets there was one moment of historical import when a young boy of eighteen clean-bowled Grace with a snorter, then slipped away into the crowd. 'Who bowled that?' thundered the great man.[5] The boy's name was Spofforth, later known as the 'Demon'; he was to haunt English batsmen for the next decade and a half.

England lost their first game to Victoria by an innings, despite an unbeaten 50 from Grace, who also took 10 wickets in the match. His own performance was greatly admired, but there were doubts as to whether the rest of the team were a match for the Australians. One cricket writer put it thus: 'Grace himself is an extraordinary run-getter, a perfect wonder, and worth going miles to see every day in the week . . . but he is alone . . . he is a freak of nature, a phenomenon.'[6]

Travelling within the country was an arduous business for the tourists as they struggled hundreds of miles by boat, train or coach in the searing heat to remote up-country venues. On one trip their coach was pulled by four cattle. Wherever they went, the arrival of the England team was a carnival occasion, bringing colour and excitement to the lives of isolated mining communities. The players were offered more hospitality than they could handle, which proved to be their undoing.

Agnes Grace stayed in Melbourne with friends, which was just as well, for it turned out that she was already pregnant with their first child. He collected her later for the journey to Sydney, where they had a memorable boat trip round the harbour and received warm hospitality.

In Ballarat both W.G. and his brother Fred scored centuries, but the team came unstuck on a terrible wicket in a small, gold-mining town called Stawell, where 37 wickets fell in the day. Grace's verdict was that 'the cricket was shockingly poor and the match a ludicrous farce'.[7] The local paper had another theory: 'The two true causes of the defeat of the All England XI at Stawell were bad ground and good liquor.'[8]

By now the bad feeling between the amateurs and the professionals in the party had got even worse: the pros were dissatisfied with the poor accommodation arranged for them and resented the fact that they had to appear in a one-wicket competitition on the final day while the amateurs went off shooting. The pros played while tipsy and earned a ticking-off from the captain.

Their next journey, to a seaside village called Warrnambool, was a nightmare. It took them 5¼ hours to travel 31 miles on an almost impassable track. In all, the 91-mile trip took them an exhausting 19 hours, at the end of which they were soaked. Despite this, however, the tourists won the game easily, even though Grace himself went cheaply. The fall of his wicket was greeted 'by the wildest shouts and congratulations on the part of the provincials, who screamed, leaped, rolled and turned somersaults, and hugged each other in their excess of joy'.[9] The resentful pros were again left to please the crowd on the final day with a one-wicket competition while the amateurs, Grace to the fore, went off in search of kangaroos.

The cricket was not so pleasant for the tourists when they reached Sydney, however, with a major defeat by a New South Wales XVIII. Grace made little impression with the bat but took 18 wickets in the match. After a jolly up-country fixture at Bathurst, which Mrs Grace also attended via a train journey through the Blue Mountains, the tourists returned to Melbourne for the biggest match of the tour against a joint Victoria–New South Wales side.

The temperature was over 100 degrees and the pitch was described as 'hard as a rock and smooth as a billiard table'.[10] Grace scored 73, during which he had the first of several disagreements with the umpire. These culminated in the England captain marching his players off the field in protest on the final day when an Australian batsman refused to accept an umpire's decision and the umpires refused to enforce it. Although England won easily in the end by 218 runs, Grace's action had struck a sour note. 'We have an intense distaste for bumptious and overbearing captains,' wrote one reporter.[11]

The tourists continued their winning streak in two up-country games in mining towns, where the facilities were fairly primitive and the pitches hardly fit for serious play. Then they beat Victoria, thanks to a vintage second innings century from Grace, a highlight of which was a huge hit out of the ground onto the roof of a marquee.

A 29-hour journey to Tasmania left the tourists weak and exhausted, but they still managed to win the two scheduled matches against locals who barely understood the rules of cricket. Fred Grace scored 154 in one of them, 'hitting hard and clean'. His brother, meanwhile, took advantage of the opportunity to go shooting rabbits and snakes.

More trouble with an umpire followed in Melbourne: an affronted Mr Budd walked off in protest when W.G. made his displeasure known about a dubious decision. A paper commented: 'Mr Grace frequently shows a disposition to assist umpires in their decisions, which is, to say the least, undesirable, and ought to be discouraged.'[12] The match was washed out by a thunderstorm with England on the brink of victory. The pros refused to attend the after-match dinner as a protest against the poor accommodation they had been given throughout the tour – much inferior to that of the amateurs, who were treated as gentlemen and the pros as their servants.

There was an absurd match in South Australia against a mining town, Kadina, that had no pitch worth speaking about and neither the players nor the umpires seemed to know how to play the

game. An umpire gave a batsman not out after he
had kicked his wicket over. Grace then angered his
Melbourne hosts by agreeing to play – for a
suitable cash bonus – an extra game in Adelaide
that was not on the schedule. The Melbourne
clubs regarded this as a blatant breach of his
contract with them. He thereby left a residue of
ill-will that clouded his reputation and soured his
honeymoon tour. A writer spoke for many
Australians when he said: 'It is a thousand pities
that want of tact and management on the part of
the promoters and the Eleven, or rather their
captain, has made them both unpopular.'[13] Grace
himself, however, either ignorant or oblivious of
the feelings he had left behind, wrote blandly:
'Our tour had, on the whole, been conspicuously
successful.'

When he returned to Australia, in the winter of
1891/2, it was for £3,000, twice the fee he had
commanded before. Grace was also allowed to take
his wife and two of their children, Bessie and
Charles. His fee was paid by Lord Sheffield, an
English peer who backed the tour financially and
was to give his name to Australia's inter-state
competition, the Sheffield Shield. The Australians

were keen to have the tour because public interest in cricket, which had boomed in the 1870s, was in decline. Grace's presence, even at the age of forty-three, was seen as essential to its success.

The party took five weeks to reach Adelaide in the SS *Arcadia*. Grace was voted 'the merriest heart on board' after taking part in a minstrel show, all blacked up for the part.[14]

When it came to the cricket, the tourists could argue that they won every match except two. The trouble was that the two they lost were Test matches, which meant that they lost the three-match series.

Grace considered it the strongest England side ever to tour Australia, which doubled his disappointment at losing. His opinion seemed to be borne out by early victories over South Australia, New South Wales and Victoria, against whom he made his best score of the tour, 159 not out. Although he suffered much criticism from the Australian press on the tour for what they saw as his imperial high-handedness, especially over umpires, the Champion was still held in awe as a batsman. One writer painted this description in Melbourne:

As he walked from the MCC pavilion to the practice nets, he looked what he is, the king of cricketers, and the personification of robust health and manly strength and vigour. With his flannels on, his giant-like proportions were seen to the fullest advantage, and an old cricketer who saw him here 18 years ago remarked 'Why, he is just the same as ever, except that his chest has slipped down a little.'[15]

One example of his high-handedness was his refusal to come off for the tea interval against Victoria when he was in full flow with the bat. He stood his ground at the crease and the umpires were powerless to gainsay him. The *Australasian* wrote of this innings:

> Dr Grace's cutting was masterful and his timing and placing up to his best form. He is, of course, not as quick on his feet as he used to be. . . . Taken altogether his display was admirable, and showed that he is still a perfect master of the art of batting, notwithstanding his age and weight.[16]

The tourists again made a number of trips up-country. The railways had greatly improved over the previous two decades and travelling was no longer the gruelling nightmare it had been before. W.G.

took every opportunity to go fishing or shooting on these expeditions.

He was in constant conflict over umpiring decisions and fielding substitutions, causing great annoyance to his hosts. He either objected to particular umpires standing or challenged their verdicts. On one occasion he said loudly: 'I wish you would pay attention to the game. We all heard the catch.'[17] Understandably, the umpire refused to stand in the second innings.

Every time he was out the crowd would go mad. The *Australasian* reported from the Sydney Test: 'The air was thick with hats and rent with shouting. Such a scene has, perhaps, never been witnessed on the ground before as followed the downfall of the England captain.'[18] At Adelaide, scene of the final Test, he boycotted an official function because he could not get his way over siting the boundaries. He also objected to the umpire and made himself difficult throughout the game, complaining when the umpires came off for rain – and when they did not. He was booed by the crowd whenever he touched the ball in the field. Tom Horan, a former Australian player turned journalist, wrote: 'Grace seems to have developed a condition of captiousness, fussiness and and nastiness strongly to be deplored.'[19]

He had his revenge, however, scoring 58 himself and winning the Test by an innings. Although England had lost the series and Grace himself had left under a cloud, never to return to Australia, the tour had achieved its main purpose and, according to Horan, Grace's visit had 'caused a cricket revival'.[20] The curmudgeon had earned his corn.

SEVEN

THE NOBLEST
ROMAN, 1878–98

Fourteen years before the second journey to the southern hemisphere, in 1878, while W.G. was revising for his finals, the Australians had made their first trip in the opposite direction. It was the quality of the Australian team on this tour, many believe, that persuaded him that there were still fresh challenges to meet on the cricket field before he could think of retiring to his West Country medical practice.

There were no Test matches, but the match with MCC at Lord's was treated like one. It turned out to be one of the most extraordinary games ever played. After rain on the first morning, the sun came out and dried the wicket and then went in again, creating an unplayable pitch. It was all over in one day. MCC were all out for 33, the Australians for 41. The MCC made 19 in their second innings, leaving the Australians to score 12 to win the match by 9 wickets. W.G. was out second ball in both innings. Spofforth, the lanky boy who had bowled Grace in the nets in 1873, took 10 wickets for 20 runs in the match and was henceforth known as the 'Demon'. He seemed to have the great man's measure and clean-bowled him seven times. He rubbed salt in Grace's wounds by leading an Australian victory over Gloucestershire, their first-ever home defeat, taking 12 for 90 in the match and being top scorer in one innings.

Grace scored only one century that season, a slow innings of 116 at Trent Bridge. His best knock was 90 for the Gentlemen at Lord's, followed by 63 in the second innings. He was so unhappy with an lbw decision that he was heard to mutter: 'I don't fear the bowlers but I do fear the umpires.'[1] He was running between the wickets while batting for Gloucestershire against Surrey when the ball was thrown in and lodged in his shirt. He ran six, three of them with the ball trapped in his clothing, before the opposing captain, Henry Jupp, asked him to hand it over. He declined, for he knew he might have been given out for handling the ball.

By his standards it was not a great season, but he was one of only two batsmen to score 1,000 runs and he completed the 'double' with 152 wickets.

For the next four seasons he played in fewer first-class matches as he settled into his medical career, and failed to score 1,000 runs, ending a run of ten successive years when he had achieved that target. He had topped the national batting averages for every year but one (1875) in the 1870s and he was top again in 1880, but that was the last time.

The year 1880 saw the first Test match on English soil. W.G. appeared against Australia with his brothers E.M. and G.F., the only time three brothers have ever appeared in the same Test match. It was not only the first, but also one of the most exciting Tests ever played in this country.

W.G. opened the England batting with E.M. and they just missed a century partnership, scoring 91 runs before E.M. was out for 36. W.G. went on to score 152 runs on his Test match début in a total of 420. Australia were all out for 149 and were forced to follow on. When they collapsed to 14 runs for 3 wickets in their second innings, the result seemed a formality. But their captain, W.L. Murdoch, had other ideas. Grace bet him a sovereign that he could not better his own score – but the Australian managed it by one run. He wore the sovereign round his neck for the rest of his life and the two men became good friends, W.G. rating Murdoch's innings of 153 not out one of the finest he ever saw.

England, only needing 57 in their second innings, were so confident of victory that they didn't bother sending in W.G. and E.M. to open the batting, trusting young Fred (G.F.), who repaid this confidence with his second duck, known in modern parlance as a 'pair'. England slipped to 31 for 5 before W.G., batting at number seven, saw them home. Not only had he scored the first runs of the first Test match on English soil, but he made the winning hit as well.

Despite his failures with the bat, Fred made his mark with a memorable catch, running round to the gasometer at the Vauxhall end to wait for what seemed an eternity under a steepling hit by the Australian giant, George Bonnor, that was said to have travelled for 115 yards.

For E.M. and G.F. Grace, it was to be their only Test appearance – E.M. because he was past his prime, G.F. because he was to die tragically two weeks later. Only twenty-nine, he was on his way to a benefit match at Winchester when he was taken ill. A chill, probably caused by playing in the rain then sleeping in damp sheets, brought congestion of the lungs that proved fatal in those days before antibiotics. He died at the Red Lion Hotel in Basingstoke.

Fred was an attacking batsman, a fast round-arm bowler and, after E.M.'s decline, probably the best fielder in England, taking many catches in the deep off W.G.'s bowling. He played with W.G. more than any of the brothers. Until his death he had appeared in every one of Gloucestershire's county matches for ten years since the county was founded in 1870, more than W.G. himself.

He was a popular, engaging personality, the best-looking and most charming of the Graces. His death caused deep shock in the cricket world. Around 3,000 people attended his funeral at Downend, and the vicar, the Revd John Dann, who was married to Fred's sister Blanche and had earlier been tutor to W.G., broke down in tears during his address.

Although W.G. played few matches in 1881, he scored two first-class centuries. One of exactly 100 for the Gentlemen at Lord's was said to be as good as any he ever played. A massive 182 for Gloucestershire at Trent Bridge was marred by the manner of his dismissal – obstruction of the field.

The next season, 1882, he was laid low by mumps until late in the season, but recovered just in time to face the Australian tourists again, now with Spofforth included. He scored 61 and 32 against them for the Gentlemen and 77 (plus 12 wickets) for Gloucestershire. In the Oval Test match, however, he was bowled by Spofforth for 4 and got himself out for 32 in the second innings when England needed him to save the game. They lost by 7 runs, the 'Demon' Spofforth taking 14 wickets in the match. Grace grumbled: 'I left six men to get 32 runs and they couldn't get 'em.'[2]

By this time he preferred to play only home matches for Gloucestershire to minimise the time away from his medical practice. In 1883 he even missed his beloved Gentlemen v. Players match and made only one first-class century, near home at Clifton.

The Australians were back in 1884 and Grace made a notable impact on their tour by destroying their secret weapon, a promising new spin bowler called W.H. Cooper, of whom they had high hopes.

Lord Harris wrote: 'Everybody was eager to see what he would do, but never will [I] forget how W.G. pulverised him.'[3] Grace scored 101 and Cooper hardly played again. He hit another century against the Australians that season for the Gentlemen but achieved little in the Tests against them. His only coup was to take a catch behind the stumps while standing in for the Honourable Alfred Lyttelton, who had come on to bowl under-arm lobs.

That was the year his mother Martha died while he and E.M. were playing at Old Trafford. A.N. 'Monkey' Hornby, the Lancashire captain who abandoned the match to allow the Grace brothers to return home, was later immortalised by the refrain in a poem by Francis Thompson, 'O my Hornby and my Barlow long ago'.

Although Grace was still only thirty-five, his figure had already deteriorated. He was no longer the lithe athlete of his twenties. His mind was also distracted by his practice and by his growing family, now up to four.

But an article in the *Pall Mall Gazette* showed that he had lost none of his appetite for cricket. 'His love for the game is intense. His enthusiasm is still like that of a schoolboy, and his happy delight when his side is winning is a pleasure to see.' He told the writer: 'My defence is as good, but I can't punish the bowling as I used to . . . and can't field as well.'[4] Some descriptions of the time suggest that his bulk may have prevented him reaching the pitch of the ball as he had in his younger days, and that he was now lofting the ball more into carefully chosen gaps in the field.

The next season, just as he seemed to be sinking towards a well-earned retirement, he confounded everyone by returning to his best form, becoming the only player to complete the 'double' and putting in one of his greatest-ever performances. This was a double century for Gloucestershire against Middlesex at Clifton, 221 not out, scored after staying up all night with a difficult confinement. 'Admiration for the phenomenal endurance of the man,' wrote an onlooker, 'was greater than love of the dazzling scientific display.'[5] Grace also took 11 wickets in the match.

Sadly, he had been less successful with his medical treatment. As he put it ruefully, 'The child died and the mother died, but I saved the father.'[6]

He scored 1,688 runs in the season at an average of 43 and took 117 wickets. 'He is still, after nearly a quarter-of-a-century's hard work,' said *Lillywhite's Annual*, 'the noblest Roman of them all.'[7] He continued in this vein for several more seasons, hitting three centuries and a 94 against the 1886 Australians, who were now touring England every other year. These included 170 in the Oval Test, his highest score against the old enemy, made (it has to be said) while Spofforth was nursing an injury.

Oxford University devised a way to counter his genius by plying him with champagne and getting him drunk the night before his innings. When he looked shaky in the nets the next morning, they thought they had succeeded. Alas, no: he went in to bat and scored a century.

There was a family disgrace, however, when W.G.'s cousin, W.R. Gilbert, known as 'the Colonel', who had played with him in the Gloucestershire team for ten years and toured Australia with him, was found guilty of stealing money from the dressing-room. In accordance with the ruthless justice of the time, he was sentenced to hard labour, then exiled to Canada. The Graces managed to keep the scandal hushed up.

Grace finished the season with more runs – 1,846 – than anyone else. He topped that in 1887, Queen Victoria's jubilee year and the centenary of the MCC, reaching 2,000 runs for the first time since 1876. He slammed 92 and 183 not out for Gloucestershire against Yorkshire and then scored a hundred in each innings against Kent. He hit 116 not out for the MCC against Cambridge University at Lord's in 135 minutes and then twice made scores of 113 for his county, the first of which was described as 'simply perfect'.

When the Australians returned in 1888, Grace celebrated his fortieth birthday by hitting them for 165. That season he was finally named England captain and won the series. Why he had never been made captain before is a mystery. It is still not clear if the omission was for social reasons, because he was not considered to be a true amateur, or because there were doubts about his tactical skills. He was often criticised for keeping bowlers on too long, especially himself.

There were two more outstanding performances that summer. W.G. scored 215 not out for the county against Sussex at Brighton, the eighth double century of his career. He also made a hundred in each innings against Yorkshire at Clifton. It was the third time he had accomplished this feat and he was still the only man ever to do it.

In 1889 he scored 1,396 runs, including three centuries, at an average of 32. By this time he was heavily involved in helping to run the new Gloucestershire ground at Ashley Down and it was there that he nearly caused a public scandal. Because of its wet condition after rain he had given orders that no one could practise on the ground. He was enraged, therefore, to find some boys using it. After a row with them, in which he was apparently provoked by their truculent attitude, he struck one of the boys with a stump. This was one of several recorded instances where Grace exploded in a violent temper. They rarely lasted long. When the boy's father complained and threatened proceedings, W.G. was lucky to escape with an apology. Whether, in practice, a magistrate would have dared to punish the great man – and whether he would have accepted the umpire's verdict – can only be a matter for speculation.

In 1890 he had the third highest batting total in the country, 1,476 runs. They included only one century but three scores in the nervous nineties. He again led England to victory over Australia, scoring a match-winning 75 not out at Lord's.

His gigantic physique began to show the first serious signs of strain, with a nagging injury to his knee that nearly cost him his second tour of Australia (reported in Chapter 6) in the winter of 1891/2. The knee hampered him in the season after his return and he again failed to score a century. His nearest was 99 against Sussex. When Gloucestershire had another unsuccessful season, the committee pinned some of the blame on the captain, especially his erratic selection policy: he almost invariably chose university men over local club players. They suggested having a selection committee, but backed down when Grace threatened to resign. The problem simmered for the next few seasons as the county's fortunes failed to improve: they came bottom of the table in 1893. Grace blamed this on his consistent bad luck with the toss. He caused more head-shaking in the committee room when he introduced his son, W.G. jnr, into the county side. The boy had a good record at Clifton College, but that was really his level.

Grace was more successful with England, however, again winning the series against Australia. There was a rare mention of his fielding when he made a good running catch at third man. The

Sportsman wrote: 'Grace ran in with all the vigour and dash of his youthful days and captured the ball close to the ground.'[8]

When Cambridge failed to select his son against the MCC, Grace retaliated by naming him *for* the MCC. But the move backfired when the boy got a duck while his father scored 139. In the return match W.G. Grace jnr got another duck and W.G. Grace snr 196. The son finally won his blue and scored 40 and 28 in the varsity match. In the next year's fixture, however, he bagged a pair and returned wretchedly to the Lord's pavilion as his mother and sister shed tears on his behalf. A quiet, bespectacled man with a gift for mathematics, he lacked the robust Grace personality, perhaps because his overbearing father had squeezed it out of him. A sad figure, he died at thirty from appendicitis in 1905.

W.G. had another quiet season in 1894, making two soft centuries against Cambridge and a good one at Hastings. He also took 9 wickets against the first South African touring team. No one, not even the irrepressible optimist himself, could have foreseen the fireworks that were to follow in 1895, his second *annus mirabilis*.

The drama started against Sussex when W.G. came on to bowl as the young Indian-born prodigy, K.S. Ranjitsinhji, had reached 150. Grace bowled him with his first delivery then later raced to a hundred himself. He went on to score 1,000 runs in May, actually in 21 days, the first time this figure had ever been achieved. He also reached another historic landmark, his hundredth hundred, in the course of a massive double century, 288, for Gloucestershire against Somerset at Bristol. He was uncharacteristically nervous as he approached his century. Charles Townsend, who was batting with him at the time, recalled: 'This was the one and only time I ever saw him flustered.'⁹ He and the expectant crowd were put out of their misery when the bowler, an engaging character called Sammy Woods, threw him a gentle full toss. W.G. did not return the generous gesture, however, proceeding to tear the Somerset attack to shreds. When he reached his double century, his brother E.M. brought out a magnum of champagne. When he was out, just short of a triple century, the Somerset wicket-keeper reckoned that only four balls had beaten his bat in the entire innings.

Far from tiring him, this success simply whetted the 47-year-old's appetite, for he went on to score 257 against Kent at Gravesend – 'such an innings,' said the *Sportsman*, 'as W.G. might have played when in the zenith of his fame and before half the present generation of cricketers were born.'[10] It was a remarkable game in itself. Kent scored 470 in their first innings, Gloucestershire 443. With Gloucestershire on a roll and Kent dispirited by Grace's hitting, the home side collapsed in their second innings for 76. Gloucestershire, meaning W.G., were left a challenging target of 104 to win in an hour and a quarter. They made it with time to spare, Grace getting 73 of them without losing his wicket. 'It was a race against the clock,' said the *Sportsman*, 'in which the scythe-bearer was always a bad second.'[11] Grace had been on the field for every minute of the match. His performance excited the writer from the *Sportsman*: 'With him time seems to stand still, and he almost seems to have learned the secret of perpetual youth. He was as lively as a kitten.'[12]

He went to Lord's for his last match in May, with 847 runs already on the scoreboard. He reached the elusive target with an innings of 169 that was admired by the young Gilbert Jessop: 'Though the attack was never loose . . . he hit it when and where he liked.'[13]

With all these records falling — 1,000 runs in May and a hundred hundreds — there was a strong feeling that Grace should receive some special reward. A knighthood was mooted by some. The *Daily Telegraph*, in a hugely popular promotion campaign, urged its readers to donate a shilling to the great man. The newspaper's appeal reached £5,381, causing W.G. to send them an effusive letter of thanks, but by then the MCC and Gloucestershire CCC also felt their members should contribute. The fund finally rose to more than £9,000, representing £250,000 today. The fund did not appeal to everyone, however. Max Beerbohm produced a particularly vicious cartoon showing a funeral procession burying one of the doctor's patients, while he put the cheque in his pocket.

The *British Medical Journal* felt obliged to speak up on behalf of one of their number:

As doctors, we feel an interest in the great cricketer as a splendid example of what exercise and training, under the guidance of a knowledge of the laws of health, can do for the development and presentation of physical vigour; and as Englishmen we are proud of him as a representative of all that is best and most wholesome in manly sports.[14]

Grace was not finished yet, scoring another five centuries in the 1895 season, bringing him to nine, one less than in 1871. He had scored 2,346 runs at an average of 51, marginally down on his great year of 1876. Even so, he did not head the national batting averages, giving way to Archie MacLaren, of Lancashire, whose innings of 424 against Somerset at Taunton had beaten the previous record highest score, 344, set by Grace himself in 1876. The following season, 1896, might have been an anti-climax, but Grace continued in free-scoring form, hitting a triple century, his first for twenty years, for Gloucestershire against Sussex. A sad aspect of this innings was that W.G. chose his son, W.G. jnr, to open the batting with him, and while young Gilbert scored 1, his father got 300 more. Grace had already hit the same Sussex bowlers for a double century, 243 not out, in the sea air at Brighton, and scored two other centuries for Gloucestershire.

For England, however, he was involved in one of the most controversial episodes in the history of cricket when five of the professionals, later reduced to two, went on strike and refused to play in the Oval Test match. Those who stood out were both great players, William Gunn and George Lohmann. Their grievance concerned money. The professionals' fee for an England match was £10 and they suspected that W.G. and other so-called 'amateurs' were actually receiving more than that in expenses. The Surrey Committee felt obliged to put out a statement saying Grace received only £10 expenses. The editor of *Wisden*, Sydney Pardon, commented: 'The earnings of the players have certainly not risen in proportion to the immensely increased popularity of cricket during the last 20 years, but to represent the average professional as an ill-treated or down-trodden individual is, I think, a gross exaggeration.' Daring to mention the unmentionable, Pardon added: 'Mr W.G. Grace's position has for years, as everyone knows, been an anomalous one but "nice customs curtsey to great kings" and the work he has done in popularising cricket outweighs a hundred-fold every other consideration.'[15] And so, with barefaced Victorian hypocrisy, was a blind eye officially turned to Grace's 'shamateurism'.

At Lord's W.G. was discomposed when a ball from an Australian bowler, Ernest 'Jonah' Jones, lifted sharply, caught the handle of his bat and went right through his beard on its way to the boundary. The great man was shocked. 'Whatever are ye at?' he demanded of the bowler. Jones replied apologetically: 'Sorry, doctor, she slipped.' He recalled in later years: 'The first ball I sent whizzing through his whiskers. After that he kept hitting me off his blinking ear-'ole for four.'[16] Grace scored 66 and England won the Test easily. Australia squared the series at Old Trafford, even though Ranjitsinhji scored 154 not out, becoming the second player after Grace to score a hundred on his début for England. Ranji was now the leading batsman and headed the averages, though Grace still scored 2,000 runs.

To show that he had lost none of his old competitive edge, Grace became involved in a controversial incident at Old Trafford, when Archie MacLaren trod on his wicket and refused to walk, arguing that he had completed his shot. When the umpire sided with the batsman, W.G. spent the rest of the day grumbling in the field.

In 1897 he scored four first-class centuries, amassed 1,500 runs and took 56 wickets. He may have been on a decline from his own highest standards, but it was still a remarkable performance for a man of forty-nine.

By now a new English fast bowler had appeared on the scene, Charles Kortright of Essex, and the two men came head to head in a keen match at Leyton. This was the first time W.G. had played there and, more to the point, it was the first time the Essex men had played against him. This inexperience showed up first in their batting, which collapsed to Grace's unfamiliar bowling. He deceived them with the flight of the ball, taking 7 for 44 on a plumb batting wicket. Then he took some fierce bowling by Kortright in his stride, scoring 126.

Many years later Kortright told John Arlott: 'The Old Man made me look as simple as dirt. He wasn't attempting to hit the ball with his bat outside the off-stump, but was punching it – punching it – with his thick felt gloves through the slips, and I was bowling fairly fast then.'[17]

His second innings was more controversial. First he stood firm as the opposition claimed a caught and bowled. The umpire, George Burton, gave him out on appeal, then reversed his decision when W.G.

roared: 'What, George?'[18] The enraged Kortright then had more appeals turned down for an apparently plumb lbw and a catch behind the wicket. Then he raced in and knocked two of Grace's wickets out of the ground. As the batsman turned to go, Kortright exclaimed: 'Surely you're not going, doctor, there's still one stump standing!'[19] This made the indignant Grace all the more determined to win, which his team finally did by 1 wicket, thanks to a fine innings by Gilbert Jessop – and a £1 bonus incentive from the captain.

Then came a great day, Grace's jubilee match at Lord's, for which the Gentlemen–Players fixture had been moved to start on a Monday to coincide with his fiftieth birthday on 18 July. Special trains brought fans up from the West Country and the ground was packed. His reception was tumultuous as he stepped out from the pavilion, a grey-bearded near 20-stone giant with a red and yellow striped cap perched, rather absurdly, on his massive cranium. Not for the first time, he looked like an overgrown schoolboy. Grace wasn't really fit for the match, with injuries to a hand and a heel, but he batted valiantly for 43 and 31 not out and he and Kortright nearly saved the game with a defiant last wicket stand.

The old man was honoured with banquets every night. Sir Richard Webster, the Attorney-General, called Grace 'a great-hearted Englishman' and declared that '1848 would be celebrated not by the French Revolution or by the abdication of Louis Philippe, but for the fact of the birth of W.G. Grace'.[20] His birthday was even mentioned in the House of Commons by Arthur Balfour, later Prime Minister and a regular attender at Lord's.

It is proof of Grace's iron constitution that he appeared at Trent Bridge the very next day, and even though he was still carrying injuries, made 168 runs. He scored 109 for Gloucestershire against Somerset at Taunton, which turned out to be his last century for the county. He might have had another one, but he deliberately declared against Sussex with his score on 93, because that was the only figure he had not yet achieved in the first-class game.

Grace always had an eye on the record books and kept his biographer, F.S. Ashley-Cooper, regularly informed about every performance for the rest of his life. Now, at the age of fifty and with the roar of the public resounding in his ears, it might have seemed a natural moment to retire.

THE FINAL
TEST

I t might have been better if he had bowed out in
the glory of his jubilee, but he stayed on too long,
causing some embarrassment to both England and
Gloucestershire. England still felt obliged to select
him as captain, even though a younger generation of
batsmen, led by Ranjitsinhji, C.B. Fry, Archie
MacLaren, Tom Hayward and F.S. Jackson had
established pressing claims on his place. Grace played
his final Test match at Trent Bridge in 1899, scoring a
laboured 28 and 1. England were saved by an innings
of 93 not out by Ranji, but went on to lose the series.

Grace's fielding was now a liability, almost a joke,
as he recognised when he came off the field for the
last time for England and said breathlessly to Jackson:
'It's no use, Jacker, I shan't play again.'[1] Making his
début in Grace's last Test was the great Yorkshire all-
rounder, Wilfred Rhodes, who went on to play until

1930, when, at the age of fifty-two, he overtook Grace's record as the oldest international cricketer.

Grace did retire that year – but not from cricket. Instead, to everyone's great surprise, he gave up medicine. Far from winding down his cricketing activities, as most people had assumed, he took up an entirely new challenge that required him to uproot himself from his beloved West Country. A new job was suddenly offered to him, as Secretary and Manager of the fledgling London County Cricket Club based at Crystal Palace. Also involved in the scheme were Sir Richard Webster, the Attorney-General, who was also President of Surrey, and Sir Arthur Sullivan, the composer.

The idea was to create a new county club for the metropolis for people who lived away from Lord's and the Oval. Grace was paid £1,000 a year and he and Agnes moved to a house at Sydenham in Kent. With them they took their youngest children, Bessie and Charles, the boy securing a place at the Crystal Palace Engineering School. Bessie, however, their much-loved daughter, herself an active games player, almost immediately contracted typhoid and died. They were devastated.

The new venture was ill-starred from the beginning. For a start, Grace had blithely assumed that he could perform his new job near London and still remain captain of Gloucestershire, which was likely to become a rival club. Indeed, he played in the county's first four games as if nothing had changed.

The rumbles about Grace in the Gloucestershire committee room, which had been quietened in recent years through the efforts of his brother, E.M., the secretary, began to surface again. The committee wanted to know, reasonably enough, how often Grace would play for them. They were also concerned that he was taking Gloucestershire team-mates to play for his new club. When they wrote to him, asking him to make his intentions clear, Grace was enraged and resigned on the spot. He thundered in reply: 'I have the greatest affection for the county of my birth, but for the committee as a body, the greatest contempt.'[2]

After nearly thirty years, the link with Gloucestershire, so carefully created by his father and sustained by his brother, was finally severed. So soon after the national celebrations to mark his fiftieth birthday, he had ended his medical career and his cricket career with both county and country.

He continued to score first-class centuries for London County for several seasons, though the team were never admitted to the county championship. Grace spent much of his time persuading his old friends to turn out for the club and even inveigled his old chum and rival, Willy Murdoch, to do so when he moved to England from Australia.

Even in semi-retirement Grace could not keep out of the news. He was involved in a curious incident in 1900, playing at the non-striker's end for the South v. the North. P.F. (later Sir Pelham) Warner hit a ball back to the bowler, who knocked it on to Grace's broad back and then caught it. In 1904, he went in last man, for some reason, and scored 80 not out in a final wicket partnership of 118.

When the club lost its first-class status in 1905 it was the beginning of the end and it was wound up a few years later. Before then, however, Grace had made his peace with Gloucestershire, for whom he became a Life Member in 1902. He led London County to victory over them twice in that season, scoring 150 in one game and taking 6 for 80.

In 1906, he played against the West Indian tourists, taking the wickets of George Challenor, who went on to become a great batsman, and of Lebrun Constantine, whose celebrated son Learie was to become one of the greatest West Indian cricketers and ended his days in the House of Lords. Grace also played his last great innings, 74 for the Gentlemen at the Oval, on his fifty-eighth birthday, a remarkable feat.

He managed 1,000 runs in 1907 and played his final first-class game the following year, for the Gentlemen of England against Surrey at the Oval. On the other side in that match was Jack Hobbs, who went on to beat most of his scoring records. Grace played in a charity match on his sixtieth birthday.

He made 26 centuries for London County in minor matches between 1899 and 1908, from the age of fifty-one to sixty, scoring the last of his centuries in 1908. The London County Club was wound up that year and he and Agnes moved to Mottingham in south-east London, where he continued to play club cricket for Eltham until 1914. In his very last innings, at the age of sixty-six, he scored 69 not out against Grove Park. He had turned out for the MCC for the last time in 1913. By this time he was busy with numerous other sporting pursuits, as well as energetic gardening. This part of Kent, now swallowed up in the suburban sprawl of outer London, was then in open countryside. Grace had taken up bowls at Crystal Palace and captained England in their first-ever match against Scotland in 1903.

He never mastered golf, having started it too late, though his putting was said to be brilliant, and he and Willy Murdoch had many enjoyable and keenly contested rounds. He also played with Prince Albert of Schleswig-Holstein, a grandson of Queen Victoria, who crossed the Channel for the game. He went beagling twice a week, kept up his shooting and fishing and even took up curling, at which he became highly proficient. Visitors, many of them much younger than him, used to complain at being exhausted by the physical exertions he pressed them into over a weekend.

In 1914 he made one of his few excursions into public life, writing a letter to the *Sportsman*, proposing that the season be abandoned and that cricketers should join up.

His last recorded appearance at a cricket match was at Catford Bridge on Whit Monday 1915 at a charity game to raise money for Belgian refugees.

W.G. felt too unwell to play, but made up for his hosts' disappointment by going round the ground personally with the collecting box, which was carried on a dog's back. He also presented a bat to the man of the match.

In retirement he had dozens of visitors from the cricketing world, including Ranji and Archie MacLaren in uniform. The war upset him profoundly. He was particularly disturbed by the Zeppelin raids on London.

Then on 9 October 1915, he suffered a stroke in the garden and died two weeks later, his death officially attributed to heart failure. In photographs he appears to have aged rapidly in his sixties. Only one of the five Grace brothers, Alfred, lived to reach three score years and ten and he happened to be the only smoker among them.

Grace's funeral, on a freezing day at Elmer's End cemetery, was attended by Lords Hawke and Harris, the panjandrums of cricket, and by a uniformed Ranji, who had just lost an eye in a shooting accident. Inevitably, with the rising toll of horror in France, the public impact of W.G.'s death was muffled. The MCC produced a memorial book about him five years later and the Grace Gates at

Lord's were opened in 1923. There is no public statue of Grace, not even in Bristol, though his gigantic bearded frame has become part of English folklore.

Agnes, a gentle woman, lived on until 1930, full of happy cricketing memories. Their eldest son, Gilbert, and beloved daughter Bessie had predeceased them. The second son, Henry, became a distinguished seaman, rising to Admiral, and died in 1937. Their youngest son, Charles Butler Grace, an engineer, died the following year at the age of fifty-six. An enthusiastic club cricketer, Charles made his exit as his father might have wished, while scoring a boundary on the cricket field.

NOTES

CHAPTER ONE

1. K.S. Ranjitsinhji, *The Jubilee Book of Cricket* (Edinburgh and London, William Blackwood & Sons, 1897), p. 468.
2. *Wisden Cricketers' Almanack* (1916), p. 87.
3. Benny Green (ed.), *The Wisden Papers* (London, Stanley Paul, 1989), p. 77.
4. Quoted in Robert Low, *W.G. A Life of W.G. Grace* (London, Richard Cohen Books, 1977), p. 10.
5. *Sportsman*, 27 August 1914.
6. *The Times*, 27 October 1915.
7. A.G. Gardiner, *Pebbles on the Shore* (London, Wayfarer's Library, Dent and Sons, 1916), pp. 27–8.

CHAPTER TWO

1. Quoted in Bantock, *The Last Smyths of Ashton Court*, part 1 (1900), p. 137.
2. Quoted in Peris Jones, *Gentlemen and Players* (Bristol, 1989), p. 16.
3. W.G. Grace, *Cricketing Reminiscences and Personal Recollections* (1899), p. 7.
4. Ibid., pp. 7–8
5. W.G. Grace, *Cricket* (1891), p. 71.
6. Grace, *Reminiscences*, pp. 7–8.
7. Ibid., pp. 7–8.
8. Quoted in Low, p. 28.
9. Quoted in Kenneth Gregory (ed.), *In Celebration of Cricket* (London, Hart-Davis, 1978), pp. 15–16.
10. Low, *W.G.*, p. 19.
11. Ibid., p. 18.
12. Ibid.

Notes

CHAPTER THREE

1. Quoted in Low, *W.G.*, p. 38.
2. Quoted in A.A. Thomson, *The Great Cricketer* (London, Robert Hale, 1957), p. 193.
3. Low, *W.G.*, p. 43.
4. Ibid., p. 46.
5. Ibid., p. 47.
6. Quoted in Simon Rae, *W.G. Grace. A Life* (London, Faber & Faber, 1998), p. 449.
7. Quoted in Low, *W.G.*, p. 52.
8. Ibid., p. 54.
9. Ibid., pp. 59–60.
10. Ibid., p. 57.

CHAPTER FOUR

1. Quoted by Low, *W.G.*, p. 63.
2. Ibid., p. 63.
3. Ibid., p. 64.
4. Ibid., p. 65.
5. Ibid., p. 65.
6. Ibid., p. 74.
7. Ibid., p. 58.
8. Ibid., p. 75.
9. Ibid., p. 77.
10. Ibid., p. 78
11. Ibid., p. 79.
12. Ibid., p. 80.
13. Ibid., p. 100.
14. Ibid., p. 98.
15. Ibid., p. 133.
16. Lord Hawke, Lord Harris and Sir Home Gordon, *The Memorial Biography of Dr W.G. Grace* (London, Constable, 1919), p. 4
17. Low, *W.G.*, p. 137.
18. Ibid., p. 139.
19. Ibid., p. 138.

CHAPTER FIVE

1. Low, *W.G.*, p. 160.
2. Ibid., p. 162.
3. Quoted by P.J. Toghill, *Journal of the Royal College of Physicians of London*, vol. 31, no. 1 (January/February 1997), 97.
4. Low, *W.G.*, p. 166.
5. Ibid., p. 166.
6. Quoted by P.J. Toghill, *British Medical Journal* (15 November 1979), 1269–70.

CHAPTER SIX

1. Low, *W.G.*, p. 92.
2. Ibid., p. 88.
3. Ibid., p. 95.
4. Ibid., p. 96.
5. Ibid., p. 108.
6. Ibid., p. 114.
7. Ibid., p. 113.
8. Ibid., p. 114.
9. Ibid., pp. 115–16
10. Ibid., p. 118.
11. Ibid., p. 119.
12. Ibid., p. 123.
13. Ibid., p. 129.
14. Ibid., p. 215.
15. Ibid., p. 217.
16. Ibid., p. 219.
17. Ibid., p. 229.
18. Ibid., p. 228.
19. *Australasian*, 2 April 1892.
20. Ibid.

CHAPTER SEVEN

1. Low, *W.G.*, p. 173.
2. Ibid., p. 189.

3. Ibid., p. 190.
4. Ibid., p. 193.
5. Ibid., p. 195.
6. Rae, *W.G. Grace*, p. 249.
7. Low, *W.G.*, p. 196.
8. Ibid., p. 238.
9. Hawke et al, *Memorial Biography*, p. 250.
10. Low, *W.G.*, p. 246.
11. Ibid., p. 247.
12. Ibid., p. 247.
13. Ibid., p. 249.
14. Ibid., p. 250.
15. Green (ed.), *Wisden Papers*, pp. 76-7.
16. Low, *W.G.*, pp. 254–5.
17. Quoted in Rae, *W.G. Grace*, pp. 419–20.
18. Ibid., p. 420.
19. Ibid., p. 421.
20. Quoted in F.G. Warne, *Dr W.G. Grace: The King of Cricket* (1899). p. 41.

CHAPTER EIGHT

1. Quoted in Low, *W.G.*, p. 276.
2. Quoted in Thomson, *The Great Cricketer*, p. 114.

BIBLIOGRAPHY & ACKNOWLEDGEMENTS

I readily acknowledge a debt to previous writers on W.G. Grace, especially the following:

Grace, W.G., *Cricketing Reminiscences and Personal Recollections*, London, James Bowden, 1899.

Hawke, Lord, Lord Harris and Sir Home Gordon, *The Memorial Biography of Dr W.G. Grace*, London, Constable, 1919.

Low, Robert, *W.G. A Life of W.G. Grace*, London, Richard Cohen Books, 1977, reissued 1997.

Midwinter, Eric, *W.G. Grace*, London, George Allen & Unwin, 1981.

Rae, Simon, *W.G. Grace. A Life*, London, Faber & Faber, 1998.

Thomson, A.A., *The Great Cricketer*, London, Robert Hale, 1957.

Anyone writing on cricket is also indebted to the following indispensable works of reference:

Bailey, Philip, Philip Thorn and Peter Wynne-Thomas, *Who's Who of Cricketers*, Feltham: Newnes, Hamlyn in association with the Association of Cricket Statisticians, 1984.

Frindall, Bill (compiler and ed.), *The Wisden Book of Test Cricket, 1876–77 to 1977–78*, London, Macdonald and Jane's, 1979.

Green, Benny, *The Wisden Book of Cricketers' Lives*, London, Macdonald, Queen Anne Press, 1986.

In addition, I acknowledge the wider insights into cricket and society provided by C.L.R. James in his classic *Beyond a Boundary* (London, Century Hutchinson, 1963). I am also grateful for information on Grace's medical career supplied to the author by Dr P.J. Toghill of the Royal College of Physicians.

I owe a special word of thanks, indeed many, to my friend Bob Low for his encouragement and generosity in giving me free access to material it took him several years to research in the course of preparing his own superb biography of W.G.

Finally, other books used are:

Gardiner, A.G., *Pebbles on the Shore*, London, Wayfarer's Library, Dent & Sons, 1916.

Green, Benny (ed.), *The Wisden Papers*, London, Stanley Paul, 1989.

Gregory, Kenneth (ed.), *In Celebration of Cricket*, London, Hart-Davis, 1978.

Peris Jones, *Gentlemen and Players*, Bristol, 1989.

Ranjitsinhji, K.S., *The Jubilee Book of Cricket*, Edinburgh and London, William Blackwood & Sons, 1897.

Warne, F.G., *Dr W.G. Grace: The King of Cricket*, 1899.

Wisden Cricketers' Almanack, various years, London, John Wisden & Co.